"Full of common-sense advice ~~on spending, saving and giving,~~ *Money Counts* also offers the uncommon sense that comes from viewing life in the light of God's generous grace and his promise of eternal glory. Read this book and learn to view giving as a liberating act of worship."

TIM CHESTER, Pastor of Grace Church, Boroughbridge, Yorkshire; author of *You Can Change* and *The Busy Christian's Guide to Busyness*

"You will be inspired and stretched by this book! *Money Counts* provides insight to everyone, from those on high incomes to those not so well off and everyone in between, because it contains fantastically accessible biblical teaching about the role money should play in our lives."

MATT BARLOW, Chief Executive of Christians Against Poverty

"This insightful book reminds us of an illuminating truth often hidden under the busy surface of our daily lives—that the way we view money and wealth reveals who we really are and what we really believe. Graham Beynon skilfully mines the abundant riches of the Bible to uncover deep truths about money, reminding us that the heart of the problem is the problem of the heart. *Money Counts* will not only make you rethink how you view money, but will challenge you to rearrange the affections of your heart."

TOM NELSON, Senior Pastor, Christ Community Church, Leawood, Kansas; author of *Work Matters* and *Gospel Shaped Work*

"This is my new go-to resource to help myself, and my family, friends and Christian brothers and sisters, become better stewards of God's blessings. *Money Counts* is a gospel-rooted, sin-exposing, God-glorifying study on money and possessions that encourages us to ask wise questions before we spend, save and give away money."

JUAN SANCHEZ, Senior Pastor, High Pointe Baptist Church, Austin, Texas; author of *1 Peter For You*

"We stress about it, relax because of it, run away from it, worship it. Christians tie themselves in knots over their attitudes to money. Yet the Bible is dripping with God's wisdom to guide our hearts and our behaviour in this area. This book won't write your household budget for you or give a straight yes/no on whether to purchase that latest box set. It will go one better. It will enable you to think God's thoughts after him and give you a biblical framework for right thinking and decision-making on money matters."

ORLANDO SAER, Senior Pastor, Christ Church Southampton, UK; author of *Big God* and *Iron Sharpens Iron*

"Christians down through the ages have wrestled with money: its meaning, purpose, dangers and opportunities. Graham Beynon has produced an excellently practical, insightful, and motivational resource for helping us all grow in generosity. I enjoyed this book, found it challenging, and will be recommending it to others too. Read it, and consider how you can use the resources God has given you to invest in eternity."

JOSH MOODY, Senior Pastor, College Church, Wheaton, Illinois; author of *Journey to Joy* and *How Church can Change your Life*

GRAHAM BEYNON
MONEY COUNTS

How to handle money in your
heart and with your hands

To my parents-in-law, Gordon and Helen, who have been an example of discipleship in so many ways, but not least in their use of money.

Money Counts *How to handle money in your heart and with your hearts*
© Graham Beynon/The Good Book Company, 2016.

Published by
The Good Book Company
Tel (UK): 0333 123 0880
International: +44 (0) 208 942 0880
Email: info@thegoodbook.co.uk

Websites:
UK: www.thegoodbook.co.uk
North America: www.thegoodbook.com
Australia: www.thegoodbook.com.au
New Zealand: www.thegoodbook.co.nz

Unless indicated, all Scripture references are taken from the HOLY BIBLE, NEW INTERNATIONAL VERSION. Copyright © 2011 Biblica, Inc.™ Used by permission.

ISBN: 9781910307359

Design by André Parker

Printed in the UK

Contents

1. Getting to grips with money

How are you feeling about money right now?

Some of us would like to escape money altogether. It's a source of annoying decisions, boring lists, family arguments, and maybe paralysing anxiety. Money keeps us awake at night.

But others of us want to embrace money, rather than run from it. It is the source of new opportunities, exciting prospects, the promise of comfort, and maybe reassuring security. Money helps us sleep at night.

These are the opposing feelings we often have about money: fear and desire. Christians are not immune from such feelings and, for Christians, we can introduce an extra component: guilt. We know we should give money away, so we easily feel guilty about how much we keep and spend on ourselves. We get trapped into grudgingly giving to push back the guilt; or guiltily keeping and feeling a bit bad when we enjoy our earnings for ourselves.

Jesus offers us a better way. A way of handling money which means faith instead of fear, and a desire to honour God instead of gain for ourselves. He offers a way of being generous rather than greedy, and cheerful in our giving and spending rather than grudging or guilty.

Imagine that. Imagine contentment rather than coveting. Imagine generosity rather than grasping. Imagine peace rather than anxiety. Imagine controlling your money rather than being controlled by it. Imagine loving using money for God's glory rather than loving it for ourselves. That is what Jesus offers.

But to get there, we'll have to understand both Jesus and money better. We'll need not just some top tips on finance, but some surgery on our hearts. That may not be easy, and it will take longer to read than "Five sure-fire ways to solve your money problems". But it will be most wonderfully worth it.

The importance of money

Jesus said more about money than any other topic: more than sex, more than hell, and more than salvation. That simple fact should tell us how important it is—or rather, how important it is that we get money right. Money itself isn't actually very important at all. It is only pieces of coloured paper, stamped metal, or figures on a screen. There was a day when money was made of gold or silver and the coin you held in your hand was actually worth the amount stamped on it. But today money is a kind of IOU or promise. What's in your wallet is actually worthless.

But Jesus knew how important it was, because lots of things hide behind money. Possessions and life style. Pleasure and enjoyment. Security and assurance. Power and influence. Money is just the front man for these much more significant desires and issues.

This is why money is so significant: your view of money reveals what you think life is all about.

The board game *The Game of Life* shows us one view. You play your way through life making decisions about study, career, and investments. You are dealt various opportunities and misfortunes. And at the end of the game, how do you work out who has won? By counting up your money. The one with the most is the winner. This is the standard view in the western world today. A successful life is all about accumulation and enjoying a good standard of living. Wealth equals winning.

Jesus once spoke about a man who would have won *The Game of Life*. He was farmer who was doing well and planning an early retirement. But Jesus said that God's verdict on him was: "You fool!" (Luke 12 v 20). Jesus thought that his was a wasted life because it was a spiritually impoverished life.

Jesus said so much about money because money is not a financial issue so much as it is a spiritual issue.

The importance of money to Christians

The sixteenth century reformer Martin Luther once said that there were three stages to a person's conversion: their heart, their mind and their wallet. He recognised that often the last area of Christian life to be devoted to God is our money.

There are a number of reasons for that. One is cultural: we don't think it's polite or right to talk about money very much. We don't ask people what they earn, let alone what they give. Another reason is biblical: Jesus warned us about making our giving something we were proud of. So he told us to do it secretly (Matthew 6 v 1-4). Another reason is personal: we think it is our money. We earned it; we own it; we can do as we please with it.

Of course, all over the pages of the Bible we are reminded that everything in fact belongs to God, and everything we have should be offered to him. Our whole life is to be lived in worship of God (Romans 12 v 1); we are to love God with all of our being (Deuteronomy 6 v 5). We cannot point to any part of life and say: "Hands off God, that's mine".

We may know those truths, and yet still think "Hands off God" with our money. At most, we give some money away, and then spend what's left as we want. In other words, we are in danger of never thinking about our bank balance as Christians.

There's more to a Christian view of money than merely "giving". It's about how we view money and what our attitude is to money. That flows into how we decide what to give and where to give it; but it also affects what to spend, and what to spend it on; what to save and what to save it for.

It's worth asking: apart from possibly giving more, do we as Christians look any different to our non-Christian neighbours when it comes to how we view, and how we handle, money?

If the answer is no, then something must be wrong.

One thing that goes wrong is that we simply don't think about it, don't discuss it, and are rarely challenged on it. A friend of mine who works as a pastor said that in decades of ministry, people have come to him asking for help with all kinds of problems in their lives. There were marriage issues, parenting concerns, work pressures, relationship breakdowns, sexual sins, self-image problems, anxiety and more. But no one had ever come to him and said they had a problem with handling money. No one had ever said: "Please help me with my greed".

We may have a vague feeling that we may need to turn the volume control down on "greed". But that's about it. If you are like me, you need to think much more deeply. I am no different. Reading, thinking, and writing for this book has been good for me and challenging to me. My hope is it will be helpful to you.

The scope of money and situations

We need to be aware that once we start talking about money, the scope of the topic is huge! We're going to have to set some boundaries. We could think about social justice and care for the poor in our society and around the world. We could think about a Christian view of economics and markets. We could think about the worldwide causes of poverty. But we're not going to do any of that.

We're going to think about how you handle your money. How you view it, think about it, and use it. Behind that are issues of trusting God for provision versus anxiety over money; contentment with what we have versus a longing for more; loving God versus loving money. As we'll soon see, you can't think about money without talking about your heart.

So we're focussing on you. And you will come to this book with a unique set of circumstances regarding money—how much you have, or don't have; how you were brought up to view money; how your friends inside and outside church talk about and spend their money; and so on.

Reading this book will be:

- *students who are already in debt because of student loans*
- *young professionals who have more money than they are used to*
- *young families with one person earning who are struggling to pay the bills*
- *single parents who are on income support*
- *those who own a large house and a holiday property*
- *those in rented accommodation with no prospect of home ownership*
- *people with credit card bills they're not sure how they'll pay*
- *people with significant inheritances from parents they're not sure how they'll spend*
- *middle aged empty-nesters who discover they have more spare cash than they used to*
- *retired folk who are having to be careful on expenditure*
- *those considering earlier retirement because they can afford it*

Money is not simply an issue when you are poor or if you are rich. Money is an issue for everyone. Poor people can often be greedy, rich people can often be stingy, and middle-income people can often be both! There is no level of wealth that does not come with challenges! We all need to think about our attitude to money, no matter what our situation. What options and opportunities we have will vary, but we can all learn from Jesus when it comes to our money.

Some people reading this may need help getting out of debt or dealing with the fall-out from serious financial problems. This book isn't going to address those issues, and I'd encourage you to get help elsewhere. But do read on as well—because, even once practical situations are dealt with, we all need to get our hearts right and get good guidelines in place for the future.

Money is not bad

What is money? Put simply, it's a tool of convenience to exchange work and goods between us. We see an example of this in the Old Testament. The people needed to go up to the temple in Jerusalem and take their tithe with them to eat in the presence of God. But if they lived a long way away they could sell the animals and buy new ones when they got to Jerusalem (Deuteronomy 14 v 24-26). It was easier to carry the money than the animals.

Money is a convenient way of swapping things, like the work you do for the food you want. As such is it not wrong or bad in itself. In fact, God expects us to earn and use money:

Make it your ambition to … work with your hands, just as we told you, so that your daily life may win the respect of outsiders and so that you will not be dependent on anybody. (1 Thessalonians 4 v 11-12; see also Proverbs 10 v 4; Ephesians 4 v 28)

God expects people to be productive and provide for themselves. There is nothing ungodly about a profit margin—it is the expected result of hard work sincerely done.

It's important to say this because some people explicitly or implicitly think money is bad. The most obvious example in history is people taking vows of poverty. Owning nothing and then begging for food was thought to be more spiritual than working and earning money. But there is nothing necessarily more spiritual or pure about being poor.

The idea that money is bad is less common today, but there can still be the assumption that money is "dirty". We feel a little embarrassed about having it, especially in large quantities. Of course if we're viewing it and handling it wrongly then we should feel embarrassed, but the point is that it's not wrong in itself. It's not a necessary evil but a useful convenience.

This extends to the things that money can buy. Possessions are not wrong either: having a car, a dishwasher and a TV is not ungodly. Western culture is rampantly consumerist and we mustn't unthinkingly swim along in that stream; but the answer is not to join a commune or live on the street. We are called to live radically differently to our culture; but we are still called to live within it.

So there is nothing wrong with money and what it can buy us. The trouble is that there is something wrong with people. That's where the danger starts.

Money is dangerous

Jesus says:

> No one can serve two masters. Either you will hate the
> one and love the other, or you will be devoted to the one

and despise the other. You cannot serve both God and
Money. (Matthew 6 v 24)

The danger of money is that it becomes our master instead of
God. We'll consider this verse in more detail later, but for now
consider this: money involves a spiritual battle. It is God or
money that will rule in our hearts. Money is dangerous because
it is not simply a matter of advice and decision-making; it is not
just about budgets, careful spending, and wise investments. It
is about our hearts. It is about what we love and worship.

This is why Jesus said it was hard for the rich to enter the
kingdom of heaven (Matthew 19 v 23). This is why the apostle
Paul tells us that "greed ... is idolatry" (Colossians 3 v 5). This is
why we are told to watch out for greed (Luke 12 v 15), run away
from greed (1 Timothy 6 v 10-11) and to kill off greed (Colossians
3 v 5). This is why the love of money is the root of all kinds of
evil (1 Timothy 6 v 10). This is why money is dangerous.

It is quite frightening to think that we can love and worship
money rather than God. And none of us are immune; from
poverty to wealth, and everywhere in between, love of money is
both possible and popular.

Money can be used well

We need to very aware of the dangers of money, otherwise we're
being naïve. But that doesn't mean we need to be negative about
money. It certainly doesn't mean the answer is to ignore money
or avoid dealing with it. As with all areas of creation, the Christian
answer is not shun it but rather to learn how to use it well.

Jesus told his followers:

Use worldly wealth to gain friends for yourselves, so
that when it is gone, you will be welcomed into eternal
dwellings. (Luke 16 v 9)

That must mean there is a way to use money in a way that God approves of. That means that we can please God, glorify God, honour God, and worship God with our money. We can care for his people and extend his purposes in this world. We can use our money in a good and meaningful way. It is quite exciting to think we can use our wallets in a way that pleases God!

But before we can work out how we might do that, we need to see how it is that Money replaced our Creator as the god of so many lives and hearts.

Questions for reflection:

1. What is your instinctive feeling about money: that it is something you want or are wary of?
2. Do you think of money as "wrong" in any way? Why?
3. Do you honestly think money is dangerous? Why or why not?
4. What practical decisions do you face with regard to money?
5. Do you think of money decisions as opportunities to glorify God?

2. How money became God

Imagine you hear that someone you know has inherited a lump of money. Or that someone has landed a well-paying job. Or you discover that they are simply stinking rich.

What is your instinctive reaction? I know that I most quickly and easily feel envious. That reaction shows I think they are fortunate. I want to be in their shoes. I want the money they have because of what I think money will give me.

That sort of reaction shows that money has deceived me. It has convinced me that it is something that it is not, and can offer me something that it cannot. At that moment of envy, I'm treating money as a god.

And this is the story of how money, a convenient way to exchange work and goods, became Money-god, a deity that is loved and served.

Money deceives us

The apostle Paul writes to Timothy about money:

> Those who want to get rich fall into temptation and a trap and into many foolish and harmful desires that plunge people into ruin and destruction. (1 Timothy 6 v 9)

Paul says that the desire for more money means we fall into "temptation and a trap". We become like an animal smelling fresh meat, being drawn in, and taking a bite, only to find itself in a poacher's snare. Money lays a trap and we take the bait.

We have to get this really clear: *money is deceptive.*

This is where we must link money with a wider understanding of sin. The Bible teaches that each one of us rejects God and lives for ourselves. It is an attempt at independence from God, running life ourselves, apart from him. But it is not really independence at all. What actually happens is that as we worship idols instead. Paul puts it like this:

> For although they knew God, they neither glorified him as
> God nor gave thanks to him, but their thinking became
> futile and their foolish hearts were darkened. Although
> they claimed to be wise, they became fools and exchanged
> the glory of the immortal God for images made to look
> like a mortal human being and birds and animals and
> reptiles. (Romans 1 v 21-23)

When we turn from the true God, we will live for a fake imitation god instead. This is where money enters the room. Money is one the false gods we can turn to. Money offers us life apart from God and independence of God. Money draws us to worship it and depend on it, rather than God. Money starts to grip our hearts.

There are two main lies Money-god peddles to us. The first is this: money offers us life now. It tells us that life is about what we have and enjoy now. It offers the lifestyle we want, the possessions we desire, and the pleasures we seek. It promises us life now apart from God.

This leads us to wanting money, otherwise known as greed. We become those "who want to get rich" (1 Timothy 6 v 9), who are "eager for money" (v 10). The idea is that people are reaching out for money, always wanting more of it. Money is the prize these people have set their hearts on because of what they think it will give them.

And, Paul says, "greed is ... idolatry" (Colossians 3 v 5). It's not simply a financial issue, it is a worship issue. We look to it instead of God. We are greedy because we look to money as a source of satisfaction, enjoyment, fulfilment, or pleasure. It has gripped our hearts and become the centre of life.

But that is to be deceived. Looking to money like this is to worship a fake god. Its message is a lie. Jesus said: "Life does not consist in an abundance of possessions" (Luke 12 v 15). Life is not about what you own.

At one level, we know that. People say: "There's more to life than money". All of us will know plenty of very wealthy people who are thoroughly unhappy; and many people who don't have much, and yet are content with life. We know winning the lottery won't necessarily make us happy or solve our problems. But we still feel like it might. That's why I have that instinctive feeling of envy over other people having money. It's because at some level I think life consists in what we have, and I've just found out they have more than me.

We are greedy for more money because we believe money will bring us life now. We have believed the lie and been deceived.

A second deception

The second lie of Money-god is this: it offers us security for the future. We so easily think we are safe because we've got money in the bank, own our house, or have a good pension plan. Money offers us security apart from God.

This leads us to trusting money. We depend on it and look to it for support and safety:

> The wealth of the rich is their fortified city;
> they imagine it a wall too high to scale. (Proverbs 18 v 11)

Do you see the picture? The rich think their money will protect them. Just like the city walls will fend off attackers, so money will fend off anything life throws at us. So we trust money instead of God.

The Bible makes clear that we will trust money or God; we cannot trust both. So in the psalms we read:

> Here now is the man
>   who did not make God his stronghold
> but trusted in his great wealth
>   and grew strong by destroying others! (Psalm 52 v 7)

We all have a stronghold. It might be God; or it might be our "great wealth". And this issue is one of faithfulness, if we are a believer. Job describes why he does not trust his wealth this way:

> If I have put my trust in gold
>   or said to pure gold, "You are my security,"
> if I have rejoiced over my great wealth,
>   the fortune my hands had gained. ...
> then these also would be sins to be judged,
>   for I would have been unfaithful to God on high.
>
> (Job 31 v 24-25, 28)

So Money-god doesn't just tell us it will bring life now apart from God; it also whispers promises of safety for the future. If you have lots of money, you'll know that there is this tendency to put your hope in it. *I'll be OK because I've got X amount in the bank,* we think to ourselves. When something goes wrong, our first thought is to spend some money, not to pray. And the fact is that it's not just the wealthy who fall for this: we can dream of having more of it and believe that only that way can we feel, and be, secure.

This is the lie sold in pension and life insurance adverts. Whatever trouble lies ahead, they suggest, you'll be fine, because you've got our special deal. What will that deal do? It will give you money in the face of disaster, when there's an accident, or when you stop working. They ask us to put our hope in money. Pensions and insurance are not wrong to have and we'll come back to them later, but the heart temptation is to think you are safe because you have them.

There is a biblical connection we should pick up on here. Poverty and riches keep their own company. Riches go hand-in-hand with self-sufficiency and arrogance, whereas poverty usually hangs out with dependence and humility. In the psalms there is often reference to the poor who trust God; their poverty makes them aware of their need. But the rich so easily think of themselves as self-sufficient. There's not a necessary link between the two—they are trends not tight connections. But the trend is seen time and again.

So do you see how Money-god deceives us? It offers us life now and security for what will come. It offers itself as a false god. It appeals to our desire for independence from God and living for ourselves.

Christians of course know these things. We know quality life now is not determined by the size of our TV. We know a good pension scheme doesn't guarantee our future. And yet we still believe the lies. One of the great dangers for Christians is to believe God has sorted forgiveness, but not living life now. We can believe God has sorted heaven, but not our old age. And so we can believe in Jesus but still believe the deceptive lies of money.

Money dominates us

Money deceives us and that leads to it dominating us. Remember:

> No one can serve two masters. Either you will hate the
> one and love the other, or you will be devoted to the one
> and despise the other. You cannot serve both God and
> Money. (Matthew 6 v 24)

Jesus assumes we live life serving something or someone. We live with a functional "master" or "boss", someone or something who is over us. That master shapes what's important to us, guides the way we live, and rules the decisions we make. They tell us what to do to get them or to keep them, and we serve them.

Do you see that Jesus views these two masters as utterly opposed? Sometimes people end up in a job where they have two line managers. They'll usually complain that each boss wants different things and gives them different work to do. The result is feeling pulled in different directions. That is the picture Jesus paints here—except that unlike some work situations, with God and money there isn't any overlap between them. They pull in completely opposite directions. Whenever you serve the agenda of money, you are pulling against the agenda of God. Opposition between them doesn't come into play only occasionally. You cannot serve God and money! It is impossible.

We've already seen why this impossibility exists. It's because God and money are operating with totally different views of life. Money-god views life as all about here and now, what you have and enjoy. It revolves around you and your comforts. It is utterly opposed to God and his agenda.

This means that when we are deceived by money we end up dominated by money and serving money. It rules over us.

An early bishop called Ambrose of Milan made this point in a sermon on 1 Kings 21:

> *"A possession ought to belong to the possessor, not the possessor to the possession. Whosoever, therefore, does not use his inheritance as a possession, who does not know how to give and distribute to the poor, he is the servant of his wealth, not its master; because like a servant he watches over the wealth of another and not like a master does he use it of his own. Hence, in an outlook of this kind we say that the man belongs to his riches, not the riches to the man."*

None of us tends to think like that. We think we're using money, but actually it is using us. It is in charge of us, not us of it.

Money disappoints us

Money deceives us with its promises and dominates us in the way we live. In a sense, that would not matter if it could deliver. But it does not; it is a rubbish master.

Money does not bring us true life now. We might be able to buy all sorts of gadgets and luxuries; we can go on nice holidays or live in a bigger house; we can wear expensive clothes and eat luxury food. But that's not what life is about. Jesus told us: life does not consist in what we have.

Quality life is wrapped up in our character, our relationships, and our living for God. Proverbs tells us:

> A good name is more desirable than great riches;
> to be esteemed is better than silver or gold.
>
> (Proverbs 22 v 1)

We should value godly character above our bank balance. Proverbs also tells us:

> Better a dish of vegetables with love than a fattened calf
> with hatred. (15 v 17)

Loving relationships are far more important than being able to afford luxury food! And again:

> How much better to get wisdom than gold, to get insight
> rather than silver! (16 v 16)

Wisdom in living is to be sought after so much more than winning the lottery.

When we look to money for life now it will always let us down, and only leave us wanting more. It is like trying to satisfy your thirst with sea-water; it looks like it will work, but it never will. This is why the writer of Ecclesiastes says:

> Whoever loves money never has enough;
>   whoever loves wealth is never satisfied with their
>   income. (Ecclesiastes 5 v 10)

We can even listen to what rich people have said. Many people have earned, won, or inherited huge sums of money. But the consistent reflection has been: "It never gave me what I thought it would". They were deceived.

Henry Smith, a Puritan minister, wrote:

> *"Riches are like painted grapes, which look as though they would
> satisfy a man, but do not slake his hunger or quench his thirst."*

Money will not guarantee security for future either. Here's what Proverbs says about the uncertainty of money:

> Cast but a glance at riches, and they are gone,
>   for they will surely sprout wings
> and fly off to the sky like an eagle. (Proverbs 23 v 5)

The various financial crashes and crunches over the years have taught us that money is not so certain, but we're still repeatedly tempted to put our trust in it. And we are just as repeatedly warned in the Bible not to do so.

Ultimately, money can never give us security in, through and after death:

> Wealth is worthless in the day of wrath,
> but righteousness delivers from death. (11 v 4)

The Bible's view of the future extends beyond old age and into eternity. And it is crystal clear that money will gain you nothing there. Psalm 49 reflects on people getting rich and enjoying life, but brings the perspective of eternity into play. Here's the conclusion:

> Do not be overawed when others grow rich,
>   when the splendour of their houses increases;
> for they will take nothing with them when they die,
>   their splendour will not descend with them.
> Though while they live they count themselves blessed—
>   and people praise you when you prosper—
> they will join those who have gone before them,
>   who will never again see the light of life.
> People who have wealth but lack understanding
>   are like the beasts that perish. (Psalm 49 v 16-20)

Money-god cannot deliver on its promises. It cannot give us fun or good relationships; it cannot secure our health or happiness; it cannot ward off anxiety or fear; it cannot comfort us or wipe away our tears; it cannot control the future; it cannot guarantee anything to us.

We need to examine our own hearts:

- *Do I really believe wealth is worthless when we stand before God?*

- *Does that shape how I think about it now?*
- *Is wisdom and godly character more valuable to me than money?*
- *Do I believe money will never satisfy but that I'll only ever want more?*

Honest answers to those questions will help us see whether, and how much, we've been deceived by money.

Money destroys us

Not only does the idol of money break its promises; it also does us harm. Earlier we saw Paul said:

> Those who want to get rich fall into temptation and a trap and into many foolish and harmful desires that plunge people into ruin and destruction. (1 Timothy 6 v 9)

The deceptive trap of money leads to "foolish and harmful desires" and these plunge people to "ruin and destruction". Wanting money will destroy us.

Paul explains this further in the next verse:

> For the love of money is a root of all kinds of evil. Some people, eager for money, have wandered from the faith and pierced themselves with many griefs.
>
> (1 Timothy 6 v 10)

Loving money is a root of all kinds of evil, not all evil. You cannot blame love of money for everything. But you can certainly blame it for a lot. Whereas we tend to think it is relatively harmless, the truth is it does awful damage.

Notice that Paul says that some people who loved money and so were eager for it have "wandered from the faith and pierced themselves with many griefs". That makes sense; you cannot serve two masters. A love of money can lead you away from faith in Jesus and wreck your life. The image Paul uses for piercing yourself is like stabbing yourself with a sword. Loving money is like a form of self-harm. Loving money can keep you from the gospel, or drag you from the gospel. It is spiritually destructive.

Do you actually believe that money could wreck you spiritually? Do you believe that money could plunge your life into destruction? This is something I have been struck by. I don't think I really believed it—which means I, and presumably others as well, hadn't really understood how dangerous money can be.

Beware the love of money

In John Bunyan's classic book *The Pilgrim's Progress* he writes of the various dangers that Christians face as they journey to heaven. There is a character called Demas on a hill called "Lucre" (money). Demas is calling people to come and join in the silver mining going on inside the hill. But we are told that when people went to look over the edge of the pit the ground was "deceitful under them and fell away". When the main character, Christian, comes to the hill, he asks Demas:

"Is not the place dangerous? Has it not hindered many in their pilgrimage?"

And Demas replies:

"Not very dangerous, except to those who are careless".

But, we're told, he blushed as he spoke. Then Christian said to his companion Hopeful:

"Let us not stir a step but still keep on our way".

That's a right view of the destructive power of money.

So when I hear of someone inheriting money, landing a well-paid job or simply being rich, how should I react? The last thing I should do is envy them! I should know how deceptive money is; how it will disappoint and dominate, and that it has the potential to destroy. What is there to envy?!

Questions for reflection

1. How would you feel if given a significant sum of money?
2. What would you instinctively think of spending it on?
3. How would you feel about giving it away?
4. How would you feel if you salary was doubled? Or halved?
5. Do you wish you had more money? Why? What would it let you do?
6. Do you think you need a financial cushion? Why?
7. What do your answers tell you about your heart attitude to money?

3. Loving the right God

We saw in the last chapter the way money can grip our hearts. It becomes an idol. We look to it to give us life now and give security for the future.

Becoming a Christian involves turning away from all such idols. Here's how Paul describes a group of people who came to trust in Jesus:

> They tell how you turned to God from idols to serve the living and true God, and to wait for his Son from heaven, whom he raised from the dead—Jesus, who rescues us from the coming wrath. (1 Thessalonians 1 v 9-10)

Notice the different elements in the change. They turned to God from idols. Rather than living for the false gods of those around them, they switched their allegiance. They changed the focus and centre of life. No longer was it the false, dead gods of their culture who they looked to and served, but the true and living God. This is the creator God, the only true God, the God who is alive.

Bound up in that change of allegiance is Jesus. These Thessalonians have put their trust in Jesus's death and resurrection to save them from the coming wrath of God. They now live life waiting for the day Jesus returns. He will come from heaven as God's ruler to bring his new creation where all God's plans will be fulfilled.

So there is a new focus to life now—they live life serving the true God. And there is a new security in life now—they wait for Jesus, their rescuer, to return.

The God of mercy

Paul lays out the new life, the Christian life, at the start of Romans 12:

> Therefore, I urge you, brothers and sisters, in view of God's mercy, to offer your bodies as a living sacrifice, holy and pleasing to God—this is your true and proper worship. (Romans 12 v 1)

He is going to go on to describe this new life as one of "worship", but before we get there, notice that this new life is "in view of God's mercy". The life of worshipping God flows from grasping all God has done for us. If we glanced back through what he's said in this letter so far, these are the sorts of things we'd grasp about that mercy.

First there's the background of our sin.

- *We have all rejected God refusing to glorify him and give him the thanks he is due (1 v 21)*
- *We are all deserving of God's wrath and cannot save ourselves (1 v 18, 3 v 20)*

Then comes God's work in Jesus:

- *God sent Jesus to die in our place to make atonement for our sin; we can now be right with God through faith in him (3 v 21-24)*
- *We can now know the wonderful blessing of forgiveness and justification (4 v 6-8)*

- *This is all by faith and so is a gift of grace, not earned or deserved (4 v 16)*
- *We now have peace with God and stand in his grace (5 v 1-2)*
- *So we can be assured of God's incredible love for us (5 v 8)*

Following from this is our new status and God's work in us now:

- *We have new life in Jesus and a new power over sin (6 v 4-7)*
- *There is no condemnation for us, only acceptance (8 v 1-2)*
- *God's Spirit is at work in us leading us to live for him (8 v 9-13)*
- *We are now God's children and free from fear (8 v 14-16)*

Finally, there's our certain future and confidence:

- *We are now co-heirs with Jesus (8 v 17)*
- *We groan now in suffering but look forward with hope to the glory to come (8 v 18-25)*
- *We know that God is working for our good even in our sufferings (8 v 28)*
- *We know that God is for us, having given us Jesus he will give us all we need (8 v 31-32)*
- *We know that nothing can ultimately harm us and nothing can separate us from God's love (8 v 35-39)*

Do you see the wonderful depths and richness of God's mercy? This is what God has done for us, and our life now is to be lived "in view of God's mercy".

This may be news to you. You may have picked this book up thinking you were a Christian, or knowing that you aren't, but one thing you have just realised is that you don't have a good "view" of God's mercy. If that's you, then more than anything else, you need to look hard and long at God's mercy, offered at the cross. Speak to a Christian friend who you know does live in light of God's mercy; or read a book outlining the Christian faith (one of the "Gospels", the accounts of Jesus' life, is a great place to start!)

The God worth loving

To live in view of God's mercy, we need to do what Paul did in his letter to the Thessalonians; compare and contrast the false gods of our culture with the true God of mercy. How does Money-god fare when put alongside the God of the Bible?

Money deceives us. It promised to give us life now and security for the future, but it was a lie. But God gives true life now, in Jesus, by his Spirit, at great cost, demonstrating wonderful love. He gives true security for the future where nothing can separate us from his love.

Money dominates us. We become enslaved to it, dancing to its tune. But Jesus is the master, 'who loved me and gave himself for me' (Galatians 2 v 20). We happily enter God's service, and discover as we do that here is true freedom, because this is what we were designed for.

Money disappoints us. It cannot keep its promises. But God always comes through. His promises are true and certain, and having given us his only Son, he will never let us down.

Money destroys us. It is a trap which will only ever do us harm. But God is the one who graciously gives us life and will only ever do us good.

Which one do you want as *your* god?

The point is that it is not only wrong to love money, but that it's a terrible thing to love. It's not only right to love God, but he is the God who is wonderfully worth loving.

Consider: What did money ever do for you? Did it create you? Does it give you life? Does it love you? Does it provide for you? Did it ever make a sacrifice for you? Can it guarantee anything for you? Can it comfort you in sorrow or give hope for the future?

No—and so worshipping money can only let you down and do you harm. But the true God has done all these things and more.

Becoming a Christian, and continuing as a Christian, involves turning away from the false gods we have loved and served and trusted. But it also, wonderfully, means turning to God, because he is good and kind. We don't turn away from the false promises of idols to a dour and demanding God who burdens us, but to the God who loves us. And so we must not only truly turn from the false gods, but turn to live for him. Otherwise we will be left half-hearted, compromised and unable to enjoy knowing and serving God.

So it is with money. We don't only want to turn away from serving money because it is deceptive and destructive, but we want to turn to a better God—the true, loving, saving God. We turn away from money which dominates and serve the God who sets us free. We shun the love of money which will destroy us, and worship the God who gives us life as it was meant to be.

The transformation of life

The mercy of God leads to Paul's call to live a transformed life worshipping God:

> Offer your bodies as a living sacrifice, holy and pleasing to God—this is your true and proper worship.
>
> (Romans 12 v 1)

Life is now lived as an act of worship to God: in all that we do, in each day of life, we are to be a living sacrifice.

This living for God means life is transformed in every part:

> Do not conform to the pattern of this world, but be
> transformed by the renewing of your mind. Then you will
> be able to test and approve what God's will is—his good,
> pleasing and perfect will. (12 v 2)

This life of worship means not living as everyone else does, not conforming to those around us. Rather our thinking about every area of life is "transformed", and as a result we live out God's good and perfect will.

So becoming a Christian is not, as many imagine, that you simply decide to add a "religious bit" to your life. That perspective sees becoming a Christian as the religious equivalent to a house extension. You're pretty happy with your house as it is, but you'd like an extra room, or a conservatory. You add on the extra room, but the rest of the house is unchanged. So people think it's similar with becoming a Christian—you add on a religious dimension to your life, but the rest of life is left as it was.

That's not what Paul is describing. He is describing knocking the whole house down and starting again. The whole structure has new foundation; every room is different. That's what it means to become a Christian. Our whole life is reordered. We are transformed by the renewing of our minds. We think differently about life.

Here the point for us: this transformation of life means a transformation of money. We think differently about money. It is not simply that I should now be a bit more generous than I was, or that I should give some money to support the work of the church. I could do those things while my view of money remains unchanged. No, my perspective of all of life has to be transformed, and that transforms my view of money and my handling of money.

- *Think how our understanding of what life is all about is transformed: life is not about how much I have and own, it's about a relationship with God.*
- *Think how our understanding of the purpose of life is transformed: life is not about me and my glory, it's about God and his glory.*
- *Think how our goals in life are transformed: life is not to be spent seeking as much fun and enjoyment now as I can manage, it's to be spent serving God as best as I can.*
- *Think how our motivations are transformed: life is not about loving pleasure, or things, or myself, it's about loving God and loving other people.*
- *Think how this changes our status: I do not need to earn money and buy possessions to gain approval or identity because I have been made rich in Jesus already.*
- *Think how this transforms our security: life is not secure because I have enough in the bank; it's secure because I have a heavenly Father who loves me.*
- *Think how this transforms our idea of a successful life: success is not achieved by gaining a certain lifestyle or income; it's achieved by pleasing my Father who loves me.*

This transformation of our thinking starts to put money in its place and gets us living for God. We don't deny the usefulness of money or the need to use money. But we start to view it and handle it rightly. We see it as a useful convenience, not an end in itself, or the means to the end of getting the possessions we "need". We see it as a way in which we can express love for God and people rather than loving it for itself. We start to honour God with our money, not honour money. We de-throne money and put God on the throne instead. We turn away from the idol of money and we serve the true and living God.

Questions for reflection

1. Do I think of God as the one worth loving and living for?
2. Do I see what a terrible god money is?
3. Have I grasped the transformation of life that becoming a Christian involves?
4. Have I assumed my view of money can stay the same?
5. Have changed my view of life, its purpose and meaning?

4. What God *doesn't* say about money

When it comes to money, God has had a lot of words put into his mouth. So as well as looking at what the wonderful, merciful, saving, real God does say, when it comes to money, we must also know what he does not say.

That could sound rather negative, but for each wrong view, there is a good and right view to replace it with. But we're going to begin with where we can go wrong.

God gives prosperity

You Need More Money is the provocative title of a book which claims to teach a Christian view of finance. It's a view which is often labelled the "prosperity gospel". It comes in a variety of forms, but the bottom line is that God blesses our obedience by making us materially better off. So live for God, and he'll make sure your bank balance goes up. It can be specifically to do with money: give money to God and watch the bank balance rise. Often it is to do with a specific person: Give to my appeal, says the prosperity preacher, and God will bless you.

A favourite prosperity gospel text is from Malachi 3:

"Will a mere mortal rob God? Yet you rob me.

"But you ask, 'How are we robbing you?'

"In tithes and offerings. You are under a curse—your whole nation—because you are robbing me. Bring the whole tithe into the storehouse, that there may be food in my house. Test me in this," says the LORD Almighty, "and see if I will not throw open the floodgates of heaven and pour out so much blessing that there will not be room enough to store it. I will prevent pests from devouring your crops, and the vines in your fields will not drop their fruit before it is ripe," says the LORD Almighty. "Then all the nations will call you blessed, for yours will be a delightful land," says the LORD Almighty. (Malachi 3 v 8-12)

God's people are "robbing him" by not bringing the tithes and offerings he had specified in the law. So God challenges their disobedience. But he also holds out a wonderful promise: if they obey him and bring the "whole tithe", then he will pour out his blessing on them: they won't have enough storage space for their harvests!

So the prosperity gospel says, honour God with your money and you will know this blessing. Of course, the flip side is that if you are not doing well financially it must be that you are disobeying God.

The great mistake of the prosperity gospel is to ignore that this promise of financial blessing comes under the old covenant. That covenant included specific promises of material blessing or punishment depending on their obedience. There would be good harvests, productive businesses, and victory in battle, or poverty, defeat and so on (see Deuteronomy 28). In Malachi, God is simply reiterating the old covenant promise.

But under this old covenant, that blessing worked on the national scale not individually. So the psalmist can see how evil people prosper (Psalm 73) and Job is example of a righteous person suffering. Even in the Old Testament there were limits to the "prosperity gospel".

But more important is the simple fact that we are not under the old covenant today! The new covenant relationship we have through Jesus does not work the same way. Jesus says his followers are blessed when they are poor, hungry, weeping, hated, excluded, insulted and rejected (Luke 6 v 20-22). You and I simply cannot, and must not, draw a line between people's obedience and their finances. Riches are not a sign of God's blessing, and poverty is not a sign of his anger (and nor is good health or illness).

Financial blessing simply is not promised to Christians today. Having said that, it is true that a general principle does remain: God will still bless our obedience. Think of Jesus' words to his followers when they said they'd left everything to follow him:

> "Truly I tell you," Jesus replied, "no one who has left home or brothers or sisters or mother or father or children or fields for me and the gospel will fail to receive a hundred times as much in this present age: homes, brothers, sisters, mothers, children and fields—along with persecutions—and in the age to come eternal life."
>
> (Mark 10 v 29-30)

Jesus is reassuring them that they will never lose out. God is no one's debtor! You cannot give to God and end up feeling like you've got the rough end of the bargain. God blesses our giving. But the question is: what sort of blessing does he give?

Jesus can't mean that if we give up our home we'll own a hundred more homes. It's hard to see how that works literally for brothers and sisters. He must mean that God will give us blessing in a hundred homes being open to us, and knowing new family in the church.

Notice also that Jesus adds we will also receive "persecutions". He is not saying that life will be one of luxurious blessing, but rather blessing alongside hardship. The point is that there is no sacrifice you can make for Jesus that you end up regretting.

So the prosperity gospel is a dangerous and malicious lie. It is most often used to put money in the pockets of certain preachers who make fake promises and point to their own wealth as a sign of God's blessing. Even when taught with integrity, it is simply unbiblical and deeply unhelpful. It is an ugly thing.

But there is a beautiful flip side. God does honour our giving. Sell your holiday home to give to mission work, and you may find yourself welcomed into many other houses. Sacrifice a holiday for the sake of church finances, and you may find greater richness in unity and love in your church. Give generously to someone in need, and you may find people giving you gifts. I use the word "may" because I don't know what sort of blessing God will give—but I know he will bless.

We can never out-give God. As he said in Malachi, "Test me in this". *Try me out, trust that it is worth giving me your money and time and energy,* says God, *and you won't be disappointed.*

God loves poverty

We mentioned in the first chapter that some Christians have viewed money negatively. Since money is so dangerous and deceitful, better simply not to have any, they say. But as a whole theology of money, this isn't right: God does not love poverty.

In fact, this is the opposite error of the prosperity gospel—it is a "poverty gospel". Not that the gospel will make you poor, but that you should be poor if you believe the gospel. It often goes under the name "asceticism". In particular periods of Christian history, ascetics deliberately denied themselves enjoyable things like certain foods, sex, or possessions. They would often withdraw from normal society and even make life deliberately uncomfortable. Some of their practices seem bizarre to us, but they were trying to reflect total devotion to God and separation from the world.

Yet while the motivation might be good, asceticism denies the goodness of creation. "Everything God created is good, and nothing is to be rejected if it is received with thanksgiving" (1 Timothy 4 v 4). God is one who "richly provides us with everything for our enjoyment" (1 Timothy 6 v 17). Food, sex, sport, music, TV, and art are not bad, and nor are money and possessions. We are not to shun them. Martin Luther wrote strongly on this in his *Lectures on Genesis*:

> "If silver and gold are things evil in themselves, then those who keep away from them deserve to be praised. But if they are good creations of God, which we can use both for the needs of our neighbour and for the glory of God, is not a person silly, yes, even unthankful to God, if he refrains from them as though they were evil?"

This is dangerous territory, because money is so dangerous. We could easily find ourselves excusing selfishness and indulgence. But the key point is to see that the answer does not lie in shunning money, but in using money rightly. We do not deny the enjoyment of good parts of creation: a quality cup of coffee, a good computer game, a decent meal out, a high-end mobile, or a relaxing holiday. Of course it can be wrong to enjoy these things—it all depends on our heart attitude. But it does not have to be wrong, because God gave us a good creation to enjoy and he remains the God who richly provides for us.

The Bible walks a fine line on this, and we must beware tipping over on either side, into a prosperity or a poverty gospel. So Jesus calls a rich young man to give everything away (Mark 10 v 21). But Jesus says it to him because he is very rich and he is holding his riches above God. This is not what Jesus says to everyone.

Paul warns the rich not to put their hope in wealth and to be generous (1 Timothy 6 v 17-18); but he does not tell them not to be rich. Paul says he's learned to live in need and in plenty—not that one is better than the other (Philippians 4 v 12).

God does want us to take pleasure in his good creation. He is the God who generously provides us with everything for our enjoyment. A godly approach to money does not justify indulgence, but neither does it outlaw enjoyment.

God approves of my approach

Perhaps you might not be tempted by the prosperity gospel or the poverty gospel. Perhaps you were sitting comfortably as you read the previous two sections. But we can easily create another category all of our own—where we believe that God likes what I do with my money. Let me explain.

Lots of factors affect our view of money and spending. Our background and upbringing will be very significant. Some will have grown up with money on hand and so presume they can buy what they like when they like (and then get caught out when they can't afford it). Others will have counted every penny, and naturally be cautious over spending (even when they have lots in the bank).

Some will have grown up never worrying about money and so will be very relaxed. Others will have known parents who were in debt. As a result they might think of debt as normal or they might have reacted against it and now refuse to buy anything on credit. Some will spend spontaneously; others only after saving up. Some of us will be frugal and others more expansive. On and on the differences will go.

So here's the danger for me: I can easily think that my particular approach is the right one, the godly one, the one that God likes. So I decide my approach, and then I conclude that (because it seems wise and good to me) God likes it. Here are three ways that I know I do this.

First, I tend to always buy clothes in the sales rather than at full price. So I can very easily make my discount approach part of godliness and look down on those who do things differently. Second, while I love watching sport, I don't pay for any sports channels. So I could easily think anyone who does is being extravagant (even while I enjoy watching a game on their TV). And third, I learned from my Dad that cars depreciate massively in their value in their first couple of years, so I've never bought a new car. I could easily make buying a new car a bad use of money.

But of course there are things I do spend money on, like drinking decent coffee or going out for a beer, that other people might consider an unnecessary luxury.

So here's the problem. We can all fall into thinking God likes what we happen to do, and then look down on other ways of doing it.

This is not easy to work out, because we're not great at noticing our own heart attitudes, and we can never fully know someone else's. So it's possible that someone else is spending or saving unwisely, or from ungodly motives. But it's equally possible that they aren't! We may be able to see what they are spending; but almost always we can't tell why.

We must not equate our personal financial decisions with godliness and use them as the yardstick by which to judge. What we need is a good deal of self-awareness and honesty, respect for other people doing things differently, and the ability to talk about financial decisions with love and straightforwardness.

It's worth asking ourselves some questions:

- *What do I consider good use of money? Why?*
- *What in my background or personality shapes my use of money?*
- *Who do I look down on for their use of money? Why?*
- *Where am I proud or self-righteous over finance?*
- *Where do I justify my financial decisions to myself and others?*

What is the positive other side of the coin (so to speak!) here? Simply that it is perfectly possible that God does like my approach because I have tried to be honest and generous and self-aware. Of course that should mean I acknowledge that God can like other people's approach as much as I like mine. Godly discipleship with money does not have to look the same for every person.

God likes financial independence

This is a tricky one, but it cuts to the foundation of how we see the world. Does God approve of the hard-working man or woman who pays their own way through life? We should begin by saying "Yes"!

People should earn their own living (2 Thessalonians 3 v 10). Proverbs also encourages us to work and earn:

All hard work brings a profit,
but mere talk leads only to poverty. (Proverbs 14 v 23)

God does approve of hard working and earning. In some circles that needs to be said, because people feel embarrassed about it.

You can probably tell that there is a "but" coming. Yes, God approves of us working and earning, but not without the right attitude. In many cultures, paying your own way is usually assumed or admired. The person who starts their own business and is successful is thought well of. The more successful, the better. We refer to them as a "self-made" man or woman.

It's not the success that's the problem; it's the view of how the world works. When God's people were going to enter the Promised Land, he gave them cautions about attitudes that could start to creep up on them unawares. Here's a key one:

> When you have eaten and are satisfied, praise the LORD
> your God for the good land he has given you. Be careful
> that you do not forget the LORD your God, failing to
> observe his commands, his laws and his decrees that I
> am giving you this day. Otherwise, when you eat and are
> satisfied, when you build fine houses and settle down,
> and when your herds and flocks grow large and your silver
> and gold increase and all you have is multiplied, then your
> heart will become proud and you will forget the LORD your
> God, who brought you out of Egypt, out of the land of
> slavery. (Deuteronomy 8 v 10-14)

The warning is clear. Once they are in the land and life is good, Israel will find it easy to "forget" God. Prosperity will lead them to become proud; they'll look to what they've earned themselves, not what they've been given by God:

> You may say to yourself, "My power and the strength
> of my hands have produced this wealth for me." But
> remember the LORD your God, for it is he who gives
> you the ability to produce wealth, and so confirms his
> covenant, which he swore to your ancestors, as it is today.
> (8 v 17-18)

Here's the key issue: whether they will recognise and praise, or deny and ignore, the source of their prosperity.

These verses come under the old covenant which included God's promises about a prosperous land to live in, but the principle still remains. All we have comes from God in the first place: our time, our energy, our gifts, the natural resources we work with, the power we use, everything.

So there is no such thing as financial independence. We are and will always remain dependent on God. As King David prays when the people have given gifts to God:

> Everything comes from you, and we have given you only
> what comes from your hand. (1 Chronicles 29 v 14)

Everything we have is from God's hand, rather than merely earned by ours. Anything we possess is from him, and anything we give to him is only returning it to him. We are never self-made.

So, yes, God does indeed like us to work and earn, and not be dependent on others if we are able to. But we must not think we are ever independent of God.

God likes big givers

It is great when people give lots of money! I mean it. It really is fantastic and I want to encourage it. Many rich Christians have done great things with their money down the years: funded the start of new churches; founded training colleges; paid for orphanages. All are fantastic.

But according to Jesus, it is just as fantastic when people give very small amounts of money:

> Jesus sat down opposite the place where the offerings
> were put and watched the crowd putting their money
> into the temple treasury. Many rich people threw in large
> amounts. But a poor widow came and put in two very

small copper coins, worth only a few pence. Calling his disciples to him, Jesus said, "Truly I tell you, this poor widow has put more into the treasury than all the others. They all gave out of their wealth; but she, out of her poverty, put in everything—all she had to live on."

(Mark 12 v 41-44)

For Jesus, the quality of the gift is not to do with how large it is. It is both to do with the proportion we give and the heart with which we give.

If that's the case, we should be pretty careful with some of the ways we speak and act. I know I can easily be impressed and think well of someone if I hear they've given a very large gift. Some churches speak about their "top givers"—meaning those who contribute the largest sums. Some mission organisations or other groups give "recognition" cards or guarantee acknowledgement of someone's name if they've given above a certain amount.

Surely this is not taking Jesus' words seriously, on two counts. First, Jesus warns against wanting any recognition for our gifts (Matthew 6 v 2-4). But second, the person who gave the least to that church or mission organisation may have "put more [in] than all the others" (Mark 12 v 43).

There is another variation on this theme of God liking big givers. That is that big gifts mean more to God. We can easily start to think we have improved our standing with God if we've given a certain amount. We can easily feel proud or self-assured because we've been generous, like the Pharisee in Jesus' story who based some of his certainty that God liked him on the fact that "I ... give a tenth of all I get" (Luke 18 v 12). We can start to think God owes us because we've given so much (which is falling into the "prosperity gospel" trap). We must beware all these tendencies in our hearts.

The wonderful upside here is that we can indeed please God and honour him with our money no matter how much of it we have. The cash-strapped single parent, the person on income support, the student, and everyone else who is struggling to make ends meet can please and honour God with their giving just as much as the financially comfortable middle-class family and the high flying business man. God notices all giving, and joyful, sacrificial giving pleases him, no matter the number on the cheque.

God doesn't mind as long as...

This is where we set ourselves (and sometimes others) a certain bar to reach or expected quota, and then say we are being godly with our money.

Perhaps the most common is: *God doesn't mind as long as... I give* 10%. Once I've given my 10%, I can do what I like with the rest of my income. The figure of 10% is chosen because of the Old Testament laws about "tithing"; we'll look at the thorny issue of how much we should give later in the book. But even if the 10% rule did apply, would that mean we could spend the rest of "our money" as we liked? Would it not be true instead to say that my discipleship should affect what we spent our money on, just as much as what we give away?

The danger of this approach is thinking that once I've ticked a certain box then God's claims on my life, my priorities and values, and what I give myself to, all evaporate in the financial world.

Here are some other examples of this approach:

God doesn't mind as long as...
   ... I'm not extravagant in what I buy.
   ... I live frugally.

... my spending is similar to those around me.

... I bank ethically.

... I give something to certain areas like my church or mission.

... I don't spend money on certain areas e.g. eating out, cable TV, designer clothes.

... I am generous with my time, home and possessions.

... I don't go into debt.

All of these can fulfil a basic requirement we have set ourselves and then give us freedom for everything else. But it is not what God says about how to handle money. It is, to be blunt, both selfish and grudging. And God has a claim on all our money, all our possessions, all our time and all energy. All our spending is part of our discipleship.

The other positive side of the coin is that we can ask how we honour God with all our money. Our whole can be dedicated to him and we can learn how our giving, spending and saving is all part of our discipleship.

Wrong thinking always leads to wrong living. That's as true with money as with anything else. Our thinking on money can go wrong in all these ways and that will change how we live. But wonderfully, the opposite is true, too: right thinking leads to right living. It is to this that we'll turn in the next chapter.

Questions for reflection

1. Where have you seen the "prosperity gospel" at work? Do you find yourself believing it?
2. Do you think it is more spiritual to be poor? Why?
3. Are there any of the "God likes my approach" ideas which resonate with you?
4. Do you think of everything we have as coming from God?
5. What's your instinctive reaction to large donations from you or others? What does that reveal?
6. Do you think God won't mind as long as... ?

5. Invest in eternity

We can use money well, but only when we don't live for it. In fact we can use money really well—but only when we're living for the life to come.

We've seen the negative side of money: it has the potential to deceive us so we need to be careful. But now we need to see the positive side. If we are not deceived and know what life is truly about then we can use money well. We can live for true treasure rather than money's fake version.

Here are the key verses from Jesus:

> Do not store up for yourselves treasures on earth, where moths and vermin destroy, and where thieves break in and steal. But store up for yourselves treasures in heaven, where moths and vermin do not destroy, and where thieves do not break in and steal. For where your treasure is, there your heart will be also. (Matthew 6 v 19-21)

A life lived before God

Before we dive into these verses, we need to know their context. Jesus is talking to his disciples about living to please God. He's spoken earlier in the same chapter about giving, praying, and fasting. In each case he has drawn a contrast between doing these things "in front of others" and in front of God. It all kicked off with this warning:

> Be careful not to practise your righteousness in front of
> others to be seen by them. If you do, you will have no
> reward from your Father in heaven. (Matthew 6 v 1)

I once heard the story of someone showing off in front of other people. He was relaying how caring and wise he had been in helping someone in church and was doing so in a way that basically said: *Aren't I great?!* As he enjoyed the feel-good factor of people's admiration, an older pastor whispered in his ear: "Enjoy it now, because you won't get anything later".

That's what Jesus is saying here: if we do righteous things in front of people so that they see how great we are, then we have lost any reward from God. So with each area of living Jesus contrasts our actions before people and before God, and in each case we are told that our Father who sees what we do "in secret" will reward us (v 4, 6, 18).

So Jesus asks us whether we live life in front of people for their praise, or in front of God for his? Do we do good things so that people will think well of us, or to please our Father in heaven?

The context, then, is about the orientation of our hearts: are they orientated to God and the ultimate reward from him, or are we focussed on what we get here and now? With that in mind, Jesus turns to money.

Banking in heaven

Jesus warns us: "Do not store up for yourselves treasures on earth" (v 19). Don't give yourself to building your bank balance and possessions. Whether it's houses, cars, DVDs, clothes, or computer games, don't focus on treasure here and now. Don't believe the *Game of Life* approach, where the person with the most money at the end wins.

Jesus tells us why not. It is because earth is "where moths and vermin destroy, and where thieves break in and steal". Old Bible translations used to say "moths and rust" destroy. That's because the word for "rust" is about eating—it could refer equally well to animals chewing the furniture or rust eating away at your car. The point is that treasure here is vulnerable and temporary. Your valued stamp collection can be stolen, as can your TV or stereo. Your designer clothes will wear out, and your car will eventually fall apart; and eventually you won't be around to enjoy them anyway.

Instead, says Jesus, store up "treasures in heaven"; because there "moths and vermin do not destroy, and ... thieves do not break in and steal" (v 20). Treasures in heaven are safe and secure. They will never fade away or be lost. It lies beyond death, and so it cannot be taken away even by death.

Jesus isn't against us storing up treasure. In fact, he expects it. You could even say he commands it. His concern is about where we are banking. His point is that banking in heaven is the only sensible option, because it is the only way to be truly secure. It is the only treasure that lasts. It is the only wise investment.

What do you treasure?

So Jesus' words are a question and challenge to us. What do we regard as true treasure? What is most important to us? That's the force of his conclusion: "For where your treasure is, there your heart will be also" (v 21).

Our hearts follow our treasure. Just like on a children's treasure hunt where we search for the treasure at the end, so our hearts run after whatever we consider most valuable. So Jesus tells you not to store up treasure on earth, because that means your heart is focussed on earth, and will become increasingly so. Your life will be consumed with what you have or don't have here and now, how comfortable and secure you are. Jesus doesn't mean we pay no attention to life now, but that must not be what we consider "treasure". That must not be what we live for. Remember the context: do we live life for we get and enjoy now, or to please God and trust him for future reward? If our treasure is on earth, our ambitions for life will be limited to life on earth; and they will rust.

Instead we should store up treasure in heaven. Consider God and his reward the most valuable thing in all the world, and then your heart will be there. We will continue to live on earth and we will take part in all of life here, but our hearts will be in heaven. In other words, our life on earth will be directed by pleasing God, by living for him, and looking forward to his reward.

This means we need to believe that God's reward in heaven is more valuable than anything we could ever own so that we live for it above all else. Ask yourself: *Is that what I really think? Do I truly believe that treasure in heaven is worth far more than anything I could have now? Would I swap my most valued possession here for treasure there?* If you do and you would, then your heart will follow.

Making deposits

But how do we make deposits in the bank of heaven? How do we "store up ... treasures in heaven"?

We do it by living for God here and now. We make deposits in heaven by focussing on what God wants us to do on earth, including how we use our money. It means we use money now as God would want, knowing that it's the best investment we'll ever make. We will think in more detail later how God wants us to use our money, but it will involve caring for people, providing for our local church, and supporting the spread of the gospel elsewhere.

We see a great example of this in the New Testament. Paul commends the Philippian church for their giving. They have been supporting him financially. He says:

> For even when I was in Thessalonica, you sent me aid
> more than once when I was in need. Not that I desire
> your gifts; what I desire is that more be credited to your
> account. (Philippians 4 v 16-17)

Paul is very thankful for the support he has received, and says so. But he doesn't want the Philippians to think he is trying to manipulate them into giving more. That's why he says, "not that I desire your gifts". Instead he desires that "more be credited to your account". He is unembarrassed to use straightforward financial language—he tells the Philippians: *You have a heavenly bank account, and every time you give money to me you are making a deposit in it.* So he desires that they might give more not for his sake, but so that their heavenly bank balance grows.

We see another example in what Paul tells Timothy to say to those who are rich:

> Command those who are rich in this present world not
> to be arrogant nor to put their hope in wealth, which is
> so uncertain, but to put their hope in God, who richly
> provides us with everything for our enjoyment. Command
> them to do good, to be rich in good deeds, and to be
> generous and willing to share. In this way they will lay
> up treasure for themselves as a firm foundation for the
> coming age, so that they may take hold of the life that is
> truly life. (1 Timothy 6 v 17-19)

He says they should:

- *not be arrogant*
- *put their hope in God not money*
- *do good*
- *be rich in good deeds*
- *be generous*
- *be willing to share*

But don't miss what the end result will be. It's there in the last sentence: "in this way they will lay up treasure for themselves" (v 19). If people with money use it this way and have these attitudes, then they will be truly rich and will take hold of the life which is truly life!

Author Randy Alcorn says in his book *The Treasure Principle*:

"You can't take it with you, but ... you can send it on ahead."

The way we "send it on ahead" is by using our money as God wants us to with a heart that wants to please him. This means that it's not enough simply to be generous. I could give lots of money away to very good causes, but be doing so to look good in front of others. And Jesus has already told me that if this is the case, I've lost any reward from God (Matthew 6 v 2-4). To put it another way:

If I give all I possess to the poor and give over my body to hardship that I may boast, but do not have love, I gain nothing. (1 Corinthians 13 v 3)

Those are remarkable words: we could give away everything we own, every last penny, but gain nothing from God. The key is why we are giving. If it's to show off, or even it's just because we can, we gain nothing. We make deposits in heaven with our money by using it to show love.

This is why God "loves a cheerful giver" (2 Corinthians 9 v 7): it is someone who genuinely wants to give, rather than someone who simply thinks they should. How can we want to give? By knowing that by doing so, we are pleasing God, and that we will not lose out when we give, rather than dreaming about how we could have spent the money on ourselves. If we think like that, then we give gladly not grudgingly, and we are making deposits in our heavenly bank account.

Seeing rightly

Back in Matthew 6 Jesus goes on to talk about our sight:

The eye is the lamp of the body. If your eyes are healthy, your whole body will be full of light. But if your eyes are unhealthy, your whole body will be full of darkness. If then the light within you is darkness, how great is that darkness! (Matthew 6 v 22-23)

Jesus words here have a simple physical meaning. If your eye is physically healthy, then your body is "full of light"; you can see properly. On the other hand, if your eyes are unhealthy, you are "full of darkness"; the world is black to you.

But that can't be Jesus' only meaning. He hasn't left his discussion of treasure to point out difficulties with physical sight, especially as he returns to money in the next verses. The key is to know that the words he uses for "healthy" and "unhealthy" have a double meaning (often shown in footnotes in English Bibles). The word for "healthy" can also mean "sincere" or "wholeheartedly". With regard to gifts or giving, it can mean "generous".

Similarly, the word for "unhealthy" can also mean "evil". Jesus later uses the same word to describe a tree bearing "bad" fruit or to describe a "wicked" generation (Matthew 7 v 18 and

12 v 39). When it's used with money, it can mean being envious or stingy (e.g. Matthew 20 v 15 and Mark 7 v 22).

So Jesus is comparing the person who is sincere and therefore generous versus the person who is evil and therefore stingy. If we are the first type of person, then our body is full of light; if the second, then it is full of darkness. This connects with storing up treasure in heaven or on earth; and, as Jesus says in the next verse, serving God or money.

So here are the sets of connections Jesus makes:

Treasures on earth	Treasures in heaven
Evil / stingy	Sincere / generous
Serving money	Serving God

Jesus talks about our eyes because he wants us to think about how we "see" the world around us; what do we see as being valuable? If we think we are seeing rightly when we store up treasure on earth, are stingy, and serve money then in fact we are mistaken, deceived, and in terrible darkness. But if we store up treasures in heaven, are generous, and serve God, then we are seeing life as it truly is, we are full of light.

Jesus is presenting us with a stark choice here. There are two types of treasure, two ways to see the world, and two masters to serve. The only question in each case is: which one will it be?

Money and the future

Jesus' words here take the future seriously. We can store up treasures in heaven which will be possessed and enjoyed in the future. We live for God's reward rather than for what we can enjoy now; it is a reward that we have to wait for.

This challenges how well we grasp the future that Jesus describes. It is a future where his kingdom will overtake the kingdom of this world, where he will be king, and where he will commend and reward his subjects. It is where this world is heading; it is the only future going, and so it is the only future worth living for.

If we grasp that, then storing up treasure in heaven is the only sensible choice. It is to see reality for what it is. But we so easily forget the future and only see what's in front of us now. We then live as if that future didn't exist and so we invest in the here and now.

This means that part of the way we counter the lure of Money-god is by regularly being reminded of the future of this world. We should remember that money and possessions will be useless on that day when Jesus returns:

Wealth is worthless in the day of wrath. (Proverbs 11 v 4)

When you finally stand before Jesus, your money and possessions will count for nothing. Whether you are a millionaire, middle income, or massively in debt, you will stand before him stripped of your wallet and credit cards. They count for nothing on that day. The person who has spent their life pursuing money will look stupid on that day.

The other way we counter the lure of Money-god is by being reminded of the reward there can be on that day.

Then your Father, who sees what is done in secret, will reward you. (Matthew 6 v 4)

But this is where we run into a tricky question: what do these rewards look like? Our problem is that Jesus spends more time reassuring us of their certainty and worth, than describing their content.

There are a few clues. Jesus tells us to "use worldly wealth to gain friends for yourselves, so that when it is gone, you will be welcomed into eternal dwellings" (Luke 16 v 9). It seems that our use of money for other people's good now means they will welcome us in the new creation. That must mean more than a handshake and a smile. Surely it means we will see something of what our money achieved and rejoice in that.

Jesus also speaks in Luke 19 about servants working for their master while he is away. On his return he rewards them. To one he says:

> Well done, my good servant! ... Because you have been trustworthy in a very small matter, take charge of ten cities. (Luke 19 v 17)

The faithful servant is given more responsibility in the master's kingdom. This pushes us on what life in the new creation involves, but clearly Jesus thinks this is a great privilege and reward.

While we might struggle with picturing the reality, what we must say is that all of our good and generous use of money and possessions, every pound we've given and every item we've lent, will count with God. Jesus wants us to know that God's reward is better than anything we could buy here, and that we will never regret any sacrifice we've made or gift we've given.

John Bunyan wrote:

> *"Whatever good thing you do for him, if done according to the word, is hid up for you as treasure in chests and coffers, to be brought out to be rewarded before both men and angels, to your eternal comfort."*

One of the cries of the modern western world is: *You only live once!* The implication is: *Make the most of it now!* This is why many of us write "bucket lists" of all the things we want to do before we die. They usually involve seeing majestic sites like the Grand Canyon, or doing interesting things like swimming with dolphins. They are all about squeezing the most out of life now.

But Jesus says there is a future life, a better life, an eternal life to come. And that must shape how we live now.

At one level, I think most Christians know this. We know we don't only live once; we know we can't take our money with us; we know that eternal treasure then is better than temporary treasure now. We know these truths in our heads. But we need to believe them in our hearts. When I give money away to God's work, do I really think that's the best investment I've ever made? When I lend my car to someone, do I really believe I can't lose out no matter how they drive it?

We will only believe what Jesus says about money if we believe what he says about the future. We need to understand what true treasure is.

So pray. Pray that you will not be so taken up with treasure here. Pray that your heart will not be drawn by all that is new and shiny and fashionable. Pray that you will know that all you possess here is fragile and temporary. Pray that you will treasure God's reward above all else, knowing it is worth so much more and will last for ever.

I don't pray that sort of prayer very much, probably because I'm too drawn to treasure here already. I've started praying it though, and can see the difference it makes. I'd encourage you to do the same.

Questions for reflection

1. In what ways do I store up treasure on earth?
2. Do I truly think treasure in heaven in worth more than treasure now? Why might we not believe this?
3. What is true treasure to me?
4. How do I feel about the idea of a "heavenly bank account"?
5. Do I believe what Jesus says about the future? How does that show in my view of, and handling of, money?

6. Guarding against greed

"Greed, for lack of a better word, is good."

That's the most famous line from the lips of Gordon Gekko, the main character in the film *Wall Street*. Played by Michael Douglas, he was based on several real-life stockbrokers and he has become a symbol for unrestrained greed. Following the financial crashes of 2007 – 2008, many people referenced Gordon Gekko in saying that we needed to learn that, in fact, "greed is good" doesn't work.

The problem is that we find it very hard to learn this. Despite all the evidence, we still so very easily think greed is good, or at least normal and inevitable. We need to learn how to guard against greed. We'll do so with the help of Jesus' words in Luke 12, where he tells a parable about a rich fool.

Wanting more money

Jesus tells his parable because of a request. Someone says to him: "Teacher, tell my brother to divide the inheritance with me" (Luke 12 v 13). We don't know if this guy had a legitimate complaint against his brother or not, but Jesus is concerned to address the issue and attitude lying behind the request:

> Jesus replied, "Man, who appointed me a judge or an
> arbiter between you?" Then he said to them, "Watch out!

Be on your guard against all kinds of greed; life does not consist in an abundance of possessions." (v 14-15)

Jesus says he's not in a position to act as a judge on this dispute, but he immediately takes the opportunity to tell people to guard themselves against all sorts of greed. Presumably, Jesus says this because he knows that this man's request is prompted by greed of some sort. And presumably he says it because he knows greed is such a temptation for everyone else listening—and for all of us.

Jesus assumes we need to guard against all kinds of greed. That is, greed comes in different varieties. There's the greed of the person who has loads, but would always like more. There's the greed of the person who has little and wants a lot. There's the greed of the person who wants a selfishly comfortable life. There's the greed of the person who is possessive rather than generous. There's the greed of the person who is constantly envious of what others have. There's the greed of the person obsessed by money, so everything in life comes with a pound or dollar sign. Jesus tells us to beware all kinds of greed.

And Jesus also assumes we will be tempted. He assumes we will have to guard ourselves. If we don't pay any attention, or put up any defences, then we will fall, and we will do so without even realising it.

So we need actively to be on guard, whoever we are and whatever our level of wealth. Greed restricts itself to no economic boundaries or salary levels. Pause for a moment to ask yourself:

- *Do I really think greed is a temptation for me?*
- *What type of greed do I most often fall into?*
- *Do I consciously guard myself against greed?*
- *What does guarding look like for me?*

What life is all about

The band ABBA wrote their song *Money, Money, Money* about how good it would be to be rich:

> "*Money, money, money*
> *Must be funny*
> *In the rich man's world*
> *Money, money, money*
> *Always sunny*
> *In the rich man's world.*"

I know it's there because it rhymes with "money", but the line "always sunny" sums it all up. Surely when you're rich it is "always sunny"? Surely life would be better if I were richer; and so surely money will get me what is good in life.

But it won't. It is not always sunny in a rich man's world. Storms strike every home, mansion and hovel. Quality life is not about how much I have. That's what Jesus means when he says: "Life does not consist in an abundance of possessions".

This challenges our perspective on reality. Put bluntly, "we brought nothing into the world, and we can take nothing out of it" (1 Timothy 6 v 7). Paul's point is the same as Christ's: life is not about what we own. If we arrive with nothing and leave with nothing then the main aim of life cannot be accumulation on the way through!

Christians don't deny the material creation; in fact we are to enjoy it. But we're not materialists. We understand there is more to life than what we see, taste, and touch. But the question is: are we functionally materialists when it comes to money?

This comes back to the deception of money we examined back in chapter 2; it lies to us about what life is really all about. This also comes back to our view of the future: we easily think life is all about enjoying the here and now. So some will spend now and get into debt. Others will save now and look forward to their future spending, or find safety in their bank balance. But it's all a version of living for this life alone. It is all thinking life consists in "an abundance of possessions".

Rich towards self

To drive this home Jesus tells them a parable. It reads like a very modern story of someone's thriving business:

> And he told them this parable: "The ground of a certain rich man yielded an abundant harvest. He thought to himself, 'What shall I do? I have no place to store my crops.'
> "Then he said, 'This is what I'll do. I will tear down my barns and build bigger ones, and there I will store my surplus grain. And I'll say to myself, "You have plenty of grain laid up for many years. Take life easy; eat, drink and be merry."'
> "But God said to him, 'You fool! This very night your life will be demanded from you. Then who will get what you have prepared for yourself?'
> "This is how it will be with whoever stores up things for themselves but is not rich towards God." (Luke 12 v 16-21)

Here's a farmer who is doing very well. He realises he can expand his business; and if he does so, he can retire early. He looks forward to saying to himself: *Take it easy*. It's going to be holiday cruises and rounds of golf for him. This man has done nothing wrong; there's no illegality going on. He has simply had the fortune of productive fields and a good business.

It's not that expanding his business is wrong. The point is that he thinks life does consist in an abundance of possessions.

He is looking to his grain to get him the money to give him the good life.

But this man has not accounted for his death. And as he begins to put his retirement plan into action, it turns out that he will not have a retirement. God says to him: "This very night your life will be demanded from you". He will put his feet up, but not in the way he was imagining. His life was meant to be just beginning, but in fact his life is over.

The original Greek makes a particularly striking comparison. The farmer speaks to his "soul". He says: "Soul, you have plenty of grain..." But then God says to him: "This very night your soul will be demanded of you". He promised his soul good things, but he will now lose his soul. And that is why God calls him a fool.

Jesus' description of him at the end is someone who "stores up things for themselves but is not rich towards God". It is someone who has been rich towards themselves but ignored God. He had plenty of treasure in his barns, but none in heaven.

Greed, then, is a symptom of a deeper problem. It runs in two directions. First, greed shows we think life is all about what we have and enjoy here and now. We are greedy because we think real life consists in an abundance of possessions. We are greedy because we've got life wrong.

But secondly, being greedy shows us we've ignored God; we've ruled him out of the question of life. We haven't acknowledged him or his claim on us. In making life about enjoying ourselves here and now, we've said it has nothing to do with God. We've been rich towards ourselves but not rich towards God.

We have to ask ourselves some hard questions:

- *What does my attitude to money and possessions say about my view of life?*
- *Does it reveal I think life is really all about what I own and enjoy, either right now or later on in this life?*

- *About what do I think: "Life would be so much better if only I had that"?*
- *Is there a part of life where I think money holds the answer?*

I don't want to assume anything about your attitude to money, but I do want to say this is an area where we can easily kid ourselves.

It is hard to work all this out, because there is nothing wrong in careful financial planning and there is nothing wrong with enjoying life. It's the attitude of our hearts that is crucial. Does our attitude reveal greed? Does it reveal we are storing up for ourselves but not God?

Being rich towards God or self can be done no matter how much or how little we have in the bank. Here's a table which lists some of the ways it might show itself:

	A "RICH TOWARDS SELF" PERSON...	A "RICH TOWARDS GOD" PERSON...
MATERIALLY RICH	Aims to gain money through a variety of means that may include overworking or dishonest business. Is selfish with money. Is discontent with what they have. Spends mainly on themselves. Is always greedy for more. Tries to avoid taxes or payments to others.	Gains money through hard work, wise investments, and the blessing of families. Spends carefully. Enjoys blessings of money but is content. Is thankful for what they have. Lives within suitable budget. Is generous and gives regularly. Pays taxes happily.
MATERIALLY POOR	Can be dishonest in work or life—steals, or deceives people to get aid. Spends beyond means. Takes out unwise loans. Hopes to gain wealth quickly and with little work. Is envious of those with more. Feels they deserve more.	Gains money through hard work. Spends carefully. Acts honestly. Avoids debt. Still gives generously, within their means. Is thankful for what they have. Would like more, but is content.

Having exposed the wrong view Jesus then turns to his disciples and tells them how they should live differently.

Remember God's provision

Then Jesus said to his disciples: "Therefore I tell you, do not worry about your life, what you will eat; or about your body, what you will wear. For life is more than food, and the body more than clothes. Consider the ravens: they do not sow or reap, they have no storeroom or barn; yet God feeds them. And how much more valuable you are than birds! Who of you by worrying can add a single hour to your life? Since you cannot do this very little thing, why do you worry about the rest?

"Consider how the wild flowers grow. They do not labour or spin. Yet I tell you, not even Solomon in all his splendour was dressed like one of these. If that is how God clothes the grass of the field, which is here today, and tomorrow is thrown into the fire, how much more will he clothe you—you of little faith! And do not set your heart on what you will eat or drink; do not worry about it. For the pagan world runs after all such things, and your Father knows that you need them. But seek his kingdom, and these things will be given to you as well."

(Luke 12 v 22-31)

Did you see the logic of Jesus' words? He says "do not worry" about your food and clothing. Why not? Because "life is more than food, and the body more than clothes". This is the truth that "life does not consist in an abundance of possessions" being expressed differently. Your life involves more than what you eat or wear, or what you own or have in the bank.

Of course, we still need food and clothing! Life might be more than these things, but it is not less. Jesus knows that. His point is not that they are not necessary, but that they are not top of the agenda. More than that, if we put God at the top of the agenda then he'll take care of the food and clothing stuff.

So Jesus points us to God's provision. First, with food, he tells us to look at the ravens who God feeds, and how much more valuable we are to God. So be sure God will feed you. Then he moves to clothing: God gives the grass amazing clothes. They are dressed more magnificently than anything King Solomon wore. Again he draws the comparison, and says: *You are worth more than grass, so how much more will God clothe you?*

Instead of running after these basic necessities, we should run after, or seek, God's kingdom. He should be top of the agenda; he should be what we are most concerned with. When we align our life with God and his kingdom, then he will give us everything we need.

Here's Jesus' call: *Live for God, and trust him to provide, both now, for the rest of your life, and eternally.*

This is why he refers to his listeners as those "of little faith"; that is how much they trust God (or don't) to provide for them.

Earlier, we examined our hearts for greed. Now we need to examine our hearts for trust:

- *Do you worry over money?*
- *Does what you need preoccupy you?*
- *What do you seek as the top priority in life?*

Jesus is challenging his disciples deeply, and he's challenging us too. It's unsettling; but there's an invitation in there as well. He is saying: *Don't you realise that you can trust God on this? Would you live your life like this, and be free of envy and greed and worry?*

A strategy against greed

So, how can we guard ourselves against greed?

First, be alert to the dangers. Have greed on your radar. Be concerned about your attitude here. We all have a "watch-out list" of areas where we know we need to be careful to live for God and not ourselves or others—sex is usually high on the list, losing our temper might make it, working hard or standing for Christ is often there, and so on. We need to add greed to that list. Be alert.

Second, remind yourself how dangerous greed is. This is crucial: if we think of greed as a low-level, petty issue we will not fight it. Underestimating your enemy is terrible tactics and usually results in losing a battle. So remind yourself:

> Those who want to get rich fall into temptation and a trap
> and into many foolish and harmful desires that plunge
> people into ruin and destruction. (1 Timothy 6 v 9)

Tell yourself that greed is dangerous, and that includes all kinds of greed; it has led people away from Christ, it has wrecked people's spiritual life, it has been many people's downfall.

Third, remind yourself how foolish greed is. This is Jesus' point in the parable of the rich farmer. The end verdict on his life from God is: "You fool!" (Luke 12 v 20). If we are focussing on what have and can gain we are being utterly stupid. It is a cliché, but you can't take it with you. Why give up so much in order to chase and gain what you cannot keep for very long?

Fourth, turn your worries to trusting God. This is what Jesus calls his disciples to do. Rather than focussing on money, focus on God and trust him to provide for you. When you find yourself worrying over the bank balance, tell yourself that there are bigger and more significant things to be concerned about. Tell yourself to keep seeking God's kingdom above all else, that you are precious to God, and that he will provide what he knows you need (though not necessarily what others, or your heart, claim you need).

Fifth, cultivate contentment. What an undervalued thing contentment is! It is fantastic. The writer to the Hebrews says:

> Keep your lives free from the love of money and be
> content with what you have, because God has said,
> "Never will I leave you; never will I forsake you."
>
> (Hebrews 13 v 5)

Contentment here is not so much the cure for love of money, as the opposite of the love of money. It is what takes its place. The cure is trusting God; that makes contentment possible. It is because God is with us and for us that we know we will have all we need. So cultivate contentment with what you have. Beware discontentment—it is the soil in which envy and greed quickly grow like bindweed. It swiftly leads to the "I deserve more" mentality, whereas contentment pours on the weed killer. Contentment dissolves those attitudes with the truth that God is with me and is giving me all I need.

Sixth, grow in thankfulness. If contentment is the most undervalued attitude, then thankfulness must come a close second. If we are thankful for what we have, then we are so much less likely to want more. If I am overwhelmed with all that God has given me in Christ, then I don't think I deserve more. A friend of mine gave his testimony soon after coming to faith in Christ. He said that before he was a Christian he wanted nothing more than to get rich, but now he realised he was rich already in Christ—and he was thankful. Paul speaks of how God "has blessed us in the heavenly realms with every spiritual blessing in Christ" (Ephesians 1 v 3). It is well worth reading Ephesians 1 v 3-14 regularly, drinking in the riches we have in Christ and will enjoy eternally, and then comparing that to what money can buy. It will make us thankful for all we have.

Last, remember how fleeting money and possessions are. Here's a great Proverb which sums it up:

> Do not wear yourself out to get rich;
>   do not trust your own cleverness.
> Cast but a glance at riches, and they are gone,
>   for they will surely sprout wings
>   and fly off to the sky like an eagle. (Proverbs 23 v 4-5)

Surely if we remembered and did these things we would "be on [our] guard against all kinds of greed" (Luke 12 v 15).

Beware our culture

Our culture wants us to be greedy—it is what drives (and sometimes crashes) our market economy. It is the way advertising works. So as we live life in our culture, we will need to beware the messages we're being given all the time. What might some of this mean in practice? Here are a few suggestions:

- *Beware browsing catalogues, magazines or websites that make you think how much better it would be to have something new. It might be for furniture, clothes, gadgets or sports equipment. Know your temptations and guard yourself.*
- *Watch how you respond to adverts. That might mean muting the TV when they come on, not clicking on a web link, or turning the page of the newspaper rather than reading the ad.*
- *Watch how you talk, especially with family members. Do you use the phrase: "Wouldn't it be nice if..."? Catch yourself*

using it, and be open to the possibility that it's a sign of underlying greed.

- Be careful in making comparisons with what friends or work colleagues have just bought, and thinking that would be nice for you. Don't think too highly of what they have.

- Consciously say thank you for what you do have, especially when tempted to think poorly of it. For example, thank God for your old but functional car when tempted to want a new one like your neighbour just bought.

- Have some catchphrases ready to say to yourself when greed shows itself. They could be key verses such as: "The love of money is a root of all kinds of evil", "Keep your lives free from the love of money" or: "Do not wear yourself out to get rich". Or they could be your own summary: Money's useful but dangerous; Life is richest when lived for God, not money; I have so much in Jesus.

Greed is *not* good. It is idolatry. It is so much better to live trusting God, and enjoying contentment. Greed may be normal, but only because we live in a world that does not seek God's kingdom. And greed is not inevitable, though you may have found yourself noticing greed in your heart that you did not realise was there. It is not inevitable because we know a God who loves us, who died for us, who is with us and who is providing all we need, eternally. There is no need to be greedy when we can trust a God who gives so much.

Questions for reflection

1. What are the most tempting forms of greed for you?
2. Are you tempted to think that life consists in what you have? How does that show itself?
3. Can you identify with any of the descriptions in the table on being rich towards self and towards God?
4. Which parts of the strategy against greed do you need to employ?
5. What practical steps will you take to do this?

7. Giving and the gospel

The financial motto of Gordon Gekko was "Greed is good". Our motto as God's people should be "Giving is good".

Everyone knows that Christians give. Visitors to church expect there to be a "collection". But why? What is the connection between giving and the gospel? What is different about Christian giving, if anything?

There is a danger that even Christians who know the gospel well simply think of giving as "something we should do". It feels more like a duty than a joy. It's something we do as little as possible. So we need to draw the line between the gospel of grace and our giving.

In Paul's second letter to the church in Corinth, he deals with this issue. He is writing about a special collection he is making, rather than regular weekly giving. He is collecting money from the churches in modern-day Greece and Turkey to give to impoverished believers back in Judea. But in describing this special collection, Paul unpacks the connection between the gospel and our giving.

Grace breeds grace in giving

Paul begins by speaking about the churches in northern Greece (the Macedonians):

> And now, brothers and sisters, we want you to know about the grace that God has given the Macedonian churches. In the midst of a very severe trial, their overflowing joy and their extreme poverty welled up in rich generosity. For I testify that they gave as much as they were able, and even beyond their ability. Entirely on their own, they urgently pleaded with us for the privilege of sharing in this service to the Lord's people. And they exceeded our expectations: they gave themselves first of all to the Lord, and then by the will of God also to us. So we urged Titus, just as he had earlier made a beginning, to bring also to completion this act of grace on your part. But since you excel in everything—in faith, in speech, in knowledge, in complete earnestness and in the love we have kindled in you—see that you also excel in this grace of giving. (2 Corinthians 8 v 1-7)

Paul wants to tell the Corinthians about the grace—the undeserved kindness—that God has given the Macedonian churches. What is this grace? It is that they have been generous in giving, even when it was really hard. It is that they pleaded for the privilege of taking part in giving, even when they weren't well off. Paul describes this to the Corinthians in order to encourage them to excel in this "grace of giving" (v 7).

So we must see first that being able to give, and give sacrificially, is a gift of God! It is a "grace" that he gives to us. That turns our ideas of giving on their head. Giving is not primarily about what I give to God but is a result of what he gives to me.

Why is that?

First, giving is a response to the grace God has shown us in Jesus. Paul explains:

> For you know the grace of our Lord Jesus Christ, that
> though he was rich, yet for your sake he became poor, so
> that you through his poverty might become rich. (v 9)

This is how God has shown grace to us—through the grace of the Lord Jesus. Paul explains it in financial terms: Jesus was rich. Think of the splendour of heaven. Think of the ongoing praise of the angels. Think of the throne of God. That is what Jesus gave up and left behind to be born as a human. Jesus became poor. He had no place to call home. He was judged, rejected, spat at, condemned, tortured. He died on a criminal's cross, watching his last possession—his clothing—being taken by soldiers. The richest One in the universe became the poorest.

Why? "So that you through his poverty might become rich". We are in spiritual poverty—alienated from God, facing judgment, unable to buy our way out of an eternity of misery. We face what Jesus took for us on the cross. So Jesus has swapped his riches for our poverty, and so has given us his spiritual riches. He has lifted us from the gutter and into glory. He became poor, so poor, in order to make us rich, unimaginably rich.

If "you know" this grace, if "you know" this supreme act of generous, sacrificial giving... then you give. Our giving is a response to God's giving to us in Jesus.

All that we do flows out of what God has done for us. We see his love towards us and so we love others; we experience his forgiveness and so we forgive others; we see his patience with us and are patient with others. So likewise we see his generosity in giving to us, and we are generous in giving to others.

Secondly, giving comes from grace because it is God's work in us which enables us to give. The verses above do not simply show us people responding to God's grace in Jesus but God continuing to show grace. The amazing example of the

Macedonian churches is because of God's grace to them: it is his gift to them that they themselves can give.

This is why Paul calls on the Corinthians to excel in this "grace of giving" (v 7). It changes everything to grasp that he doesn't call it the practice of giving or the discipline of giving, or even the rightness of giving. It is the grace of giving. It is the gift of being able to give in the light of God's gift.

So when Paul sees someone giving his observation is: *There is God's grace at work.* It's a very different way of thinking about giving. When we see someone giving money, we easily think they are being generous or sacrificial (which they are). But we don't tend also to think that God has given them grace.

When we see giving as a grace from God, done in response to the grace of God, we begin to understand why the Macedonian Christians gave as they did:

- *They pleaded for the opportunity to give rather than responding to pleas for money.*
- *They gave even when they were hard up themselves.*
- *They gave "beyond their ability": this does not necessarily mean they gave more than they could afford, but rather, more than would have been expected.*
- *They saw giving as a "privilege".*
- *Behind their willingness to give was a devotion to Jesus: "they gave themselves first of all to the Lord".*
- *This wasn't so much an act of charity but of worship: the word used for "service" to the Lord's people used to refer to service in the temple.*
- *Their giving was voluntary, done "entirely on their own".*

This is a completely different view of giving, and it all flows from knowing, deep in our hearts, "the grace of our Lord Jesus Christ". Spend a moment reflecting:

- *Would you ever think of asking for the opportunity to give?*
- *Do you think of giving as privilege or a duty?*
- *Do you think hard times would give you a reason not to give?*
- *Do you consider your giving as an act of worship to God?*

The call to give

Paul cites the example of the Macedonian churches because he wants to encourage and spur on the Corinthians. But then he goes on to call them to give in the light of the gospel. He says that he has sent Titus to "bring ... to completion this act of grace on your part" (v 6). Titus is coming to collect the offering from Corinth. Paul goes on to advise them how to proceed:

> And here is my judgment about what is best for you in this matter. Last year you were the first not only to give but also to have the desire to do so. Now finish the work, so that your eager willingness to do it may be matched by your completion of it, according to your means. For if the willingness is there, the gift is acceptable according to what one has, not according to what one does not have. (v 10-12)

Paul reminds them that previously they were the first to give and the first to want to give. Now he encourages them to finish this work—that is, to finish collecting the money they are going to give towards this particular need. He encourages them to make sure that their willingness is matched by action. I expect we all know the experience of feeling like we want to give to something, but then we need prompting to actually write the cheque. Good intentions are not always translated into actions. Paul knows this: so here he is, giving these Christians a nudge to follow through on their eagerness.

It's important to see that Paul says they should give "according to [their] means". He doesn't expect them to give money that they don't have. The last verse is the explanation: God is concerned with their willingness to give according to what they have. It's possible that the Corinthians felt they couldn't raise a suitably large amount; if so, Paul is reassuring them that that's OK. God knows what's in the bank, and he doesn't expect us to go into the overdraft. We must not think then that God ever makes unreasonable demands on us in giving. He knows what we have and what we need to live on. God is more bothered about our willingness and desire.

A desire for equality

Paul goes on to outline what he wants to be achieved by their gift:

> Our desire is not that others might be relieved while you are hard pressed, but that there might be equality. At the present time your plenty will supply what they need, so that in turn their plenty will supply what you need. The goal is equality, as it is written: "The one who gathered much did not have too much, and the one who gathered little did not have too little." (v 13-15)

Paul's desire is for "equality". He doesn't mean a kind of communist ideal of redistribution of wealth, but a Christian ideal of concern for brothers and sisters. There is plenty of evidence in the New Testament that Christians varied in their personal wealth and there was no attempt to bring everyone to the same level. Instead this is about concern when a brother or sister is in trouble that they might be relieved and no one is left in need.

So in our churches we should not be surprised that some own bigger houses than others or have more disposable income.

But what we should want is no one to be in need when others have more than they need. And of course, in this particular example Paul is talking about those in churches elsewhere. There is surely a great challenge for those of us who live in the prosperous west to relieve the need of brothers and sisters elsewhere in the world. If we have more than we need, then this should prompt us to ask whether and how God might be giving us the grace of having that "extra" in order to give it to those who need it.

Sowing and reaping

Later on, Paul expresses some simple but profound principles of giving using a farming metaphor:

> Remember this: whoever sows sparingly will also reap sparingly, and whoever sows generously will also reap generously. Each of you should give what you have decided in your heart to give, not reluctantly or under compulsion, for God loves a cheerful giver. And God is able to bless you abundantly, so that in all things at all times, having all that you need, you will abound in every good work. As it is written:
> "They have freely scattered their gifts to the poor;
> their righteousness endures for ever."
> Now he who supplies seed to the sower and bread for food will also supply and increase your store of seed and will enlarge the harvest of your righteousness. You will be enriched in every way so that you can be generous on every occasion, and through us your generosity will result in thanksgiving to God. (9 v 6-11)

Paul uses the picture of sowing and reaping to picture the idea that there is a return on our giving. The reaping is not necessarily financial, though: God blesses us so that we abound in every good work (v 8). God will increase our store of seed and our harvest of "righteousness" (v 10). God enriches us in "every way" so that we can be generous (v 11). This may well include financial return, or at least that God will look after us financially. But the central picture is simply that of God bringing his blessing.

Remember the prosperity gospel from chapter four? It is wrong in saying God will make us materially rich, but it is right in that God blesses our giving. As we give away, we must think of ourselves not so much as "giving" but "sowing"—sowing that results in reaping. We cannot out-give God. All our gifts to him result in his blessing of us.

This means that giving is a profound act of trusting. I'm not giving money away. I'm sowing in the ground and trusting there will be a harvest. That harvest may include God ensuring I have enough in the bank (so I can continue to be generous); it may be a harvest of righteousness in some other way. But as I give, I trust God will use my gift for his purposes and I will reap a reward.

And all this is an act of God's grace to us. It is not that having given, God owes us under his heavenly reward scheme. Paul says: "God is able to bless you abundantly" (v 8); a more literal translation is: "God is able to make all grace abound to you". This is not about putting God in a position where he owes us, but putting ourselves in a position where he will pour his grace upon us.

Within this description of sowing and reaping, the main thing that Paul wants to encourage is a corresponding type of giving. Paul sees God's grace as resulting in a giving that is generous, voluntary, and cheerful. What he says in verse 7 is key: "Each of you should give what you have decided in your heart to give, not reluctantly or under compulsion, for God loves a cheerful giver."

Each person is responsible to make their own decision as to how much to give. They should do so without peer pressure, leader pressure, or any other kind of compulsion. God wants us to give cheerfully, not grudgingly; because we long to, not because we have to. This is something that has been recognised down the centuries as a distinctive of true Christian giving. In his *Apology*, the early church leader Tertullian said: "Every man once a month brings some modest coin—or whenever he wishes, and only if he does wish, and if he can; for nobody is compelled; it is a voluntary offering."

Voluntary, generous, cheerful giving might seem a long way away. I most instinctively think of giving as necessary duty, not cheerful delight. That just goes to show how much I need to grow in this area. But there are moments when I grasp this. They are moments when I see that all our giving flows from God's grace to me. They are moments when I see that giving is like sowing and a harvest will come back to me. They are moments when I see that God continues to be gracious in providing everything for me. These truths flow out into giving voluntarily, generously and cheerfully. I am praying that those moments would become more regular and long-lasting, until it becomes my ongoing view.

Look at what's being achieved

Lastly, Paul encourages the Corinthians with a wonderful picture of what is being achieved by their gifts:

> This service that you perform is not only supplying the
> needs of the Lord's people but is also overflowing in
> many expressions of thanks to God. Because of the

service by which you have proved yourselves, others will praise God for the obedience that accompanies your confession of the gospel of Christ, and for your generosity in sharing with them and with everyone else. And in their prayers for you their hearts will go out to you, because of the surpassing grace God has given you. Thanks be to God for his indescribable gift! (v 12-15)

Just think what your giving is achieving, says Paul. It is meeting the needs of God's people elsewhere. More than that, it is resulting in the overflow of thanksgiving to God. Other Christians are thanking God because of what the Corinthian Christians are doing. In fact, he goes on, people will praise God for their obedience and generosity in giving. Not only that, but in their prayers for them, the recipients' "hearts will go out to you". What a wonderful picture of thanks, praise and prayer! And all because of the "surpassing grace God has given you".

We too can know this. With our giving, we can meet people's needs. With our giving, thanksgiving can go to God. With our giving, people will praise God for his work in us. With our giving, people will pray for us and their hearts will grow warm to us. And all because of God's grace to us. He could directly meet all of his people's needs. Instead, he invites some of his people to enjoy being part of the way he meets others' needs, and some of his people to enjoy receiving what they need from their brothers and sisters.

We end where we began—giving comes from grace. We might give to God, but we always end by giving thanks to him for his "indescribable gift" to us.

Giving transformed by the gospel

So what have we seen from Paul's letter to the Corinthians about giving and the gospel?

1. Giving flows from God's grace to us
2. Giving is a work of God's grace in us
3. Giving is act of worship to God
4. Giving shows care and equality for brothers and sisters
5. Giving is like sowing and we will reap accordingly to God's grace
6. Giving should be generous and voluntary
7. Giving supplies people's needs and results in praise and thanksgiving to God
8. Giving comes from God's grace in giving to us

Paul begins and ends with God's grace in giving to us, and manages to insert God's grace in the middle as well! The grace shown to us in the gospel transforms our view of giving. God's overwhelming generosity in Christ changes our hearts; it turns them outwards from selfishness, and enables us to give. God's ongoing grace in proving for us means we need not have hearts that grasp tightly to our money, but can trust him to provide for us and so bless us, as we give. God's indescribable gift to us means our hearts can genuinely want to give to others.

There is a Christian discipleship manual from the second century called *The Teaching*. Here's its comment on money:

> *"Do not be one who holds his hand out to take, but shuts it when it comes to giving ... Do not hesitate to give and do not give with a bad grace, for you will discover who he is that pays you back a reward with a good grace."*

Here's the bottom line: if we know God's generosity to us in Christ, our hands and wallets will be open, not shut. Giving is good. It is a gift.

Questions for reflection:

1. Jesus tells us it is more blessed to give than to receive. Do we believe him?
2. How do we think the gospel and giving are connected? Does anything need to change in our thinking?
3. What principles about giving do I/we need to take on board more fully?
4. What does my giving say about my understanding of grace?

8. Giving in practice

We've seen how giving is transformed by the gospel. God's grace to us flows out into our generous giving. But what does giving look like in practice?

What do we give to?

In both the Old Testament and the New Testament, we see clear examples of what money is given to.

In the Old Testament, there were rules and commands about giving to those who were poor. For example:

> If anyone is poor among your fellow Israelites in any of the towns of the land that the LORD your God is giving you, do not be hard-hearted or tight-fisted towards them. Rather, be open-handed and freely lend them whatever they need. (Deuteronomy 15 v 7-8)

It's striking that there is a focus on the poor who are fellow Israelites. However, God's people were also to care for the foreigners among them:

> When a foreigner resides among you in your land, do not ill-treat them. The foreigner residing among you must be treated as your native-born. Love them as yourself, for you were foreigners in Egypt. I am the LORD your God.
>
> (Leviticus 19 v 33-34)

There were also tithes for the support of the Levites: this was the tribe from which the priests came. The Levites were not allowed to own land, and so depended on the giving of the rest of the tribes to support them. The priests were to run the temple, instruct God's people in how to live, and oversee the devotional life of the people of God. And so the people were to support them financially:

> At the end of every three years, bring all the tithes of that year's produce and store it in your towns, so that the Levites (who have no land allotted to them or any inheritance of their own) and the foreigners, the fatherless and the widows who live in your towns may come and eat and be satisfied, and so that the LORD your God may bless you in all the work of your hands.
>
> (Deuteronomy 14 v 28-29)

This lays out the essentials of what we are to give to: we give to relieve need, and to promote God's rule or his work among his people.

We see the same thing in the New Testament. First, there is care of those in need. This is seen primarily within the church:

> All the believers were one in heart and mind. No one claimed that any of their possessions was their own, but they shared everything they had. With great power the apostles continued to testify to the resurrection of the Lord Jesus. And God's grace was so powerfully at work in them all that there was no needy person among them. For from time to time those who owned land or houses sold them, brought the money from the sales and put it at the apostles' feet, and it was distributed to anyone who had need. (Acts 4 v 32-35)

Later in Acts, there is a lovely example of God's people in one place caring for others in need in another:

> During this time some prophets came down from Jerusalem to Antioch. One of them, named Agabus, stood up and through the Spirit predicted that a severe famine would spread over the entire Roman world. (This happened during the reign of Claudius.) The disciples, as each one was able, decided to provide help for the brothers and sisters living in Judea. This they did, sending their gift to the elders by Barnabas and Saul.
>
> (Acts 11 v 27-30)

The care here is primarily within the Christian community because of the new relationship between Christians. We have been bound together as God's family—we are brothers and sisters united in Christ—and so we care for each other. We saw another example of this in Paul's collection of money in 2 Corinthians in the previous chapter. And this is expressed in that early Christian document called *The Teaching*. Speaking about money, it says:

> *"Do not turn your back on the needy, but share everything with your brother and call nothing your own. For if you have what is eternal in common, how much more should you have what is transient!"*

Care can, and should, overflow to those outside the church as well. Jesus tells us to love our enemies and to do good to them (Luke 6 v 35). So Paul says:

> Therefore, as we have opportunity, let us do good to all people, especially to those who belong to the family of believers. (Galatians 6 v 10)

Our "doing good" is to all people, but with special responsibility to those in the church. They are our family.

What will this mean in practice? Think of expanding circles of giving. There's care for those within our own church. That can be informal help: I've seen people give meals, lend cars, buy presents, do DIY, pass on clothes and more, all to care for those who aren't as well-off financially. But it can also be more organised. In Acts, the apostles oversaw the distribution of money and later responsibility for food distribution was passed on to other leaders (Acts 6 v 1-7). So today church leaderships should be aware of those struggling and organise appropriate care.

There should also be care between churches or Christians in other parts of the country or world (as we saw in Acts 11). That might be a larger church partnering with a smaller one in the same city, elsewhere in the country, or across the world. I've been in churches which have done that and have known great mutual enrichment as a result. We can also give through organisations who help persecuted or suffering Christians around the world.

Then there is care for those who are not believers but who are in our locality. I've seen churches help with food banks, debt coaching, child care, jobs clubs, housing associations and more. This takes us into the much broader areas of social involvement, but the point is that our desire to give towards care will take us there in some form or other.

Lastly, there is giving to care for non-Christians elsewhere in the world. That might be through disaster relief funds, child-sponsorship schemes, aid projects, and much more. There is so much need we can feel paralysed by it. We can't do everything; but we surely must do something. It's worth remembering that God wants us to give what we can, and is pleased when we do so cheerfully; he does not call us to give or to do what we can't.

And just as in the Old Testament, we also see in the New Testament examples of believers giving to promote God's rule and work in the world. This is seen in support of Christian workers who are spreading the message of the gospel. The first and prime example is in support of those who are set apart for leading and running of your own church. Paul says that elders are worthy of "double honour" (1 Timothy 5 v 17)—the honour of respect and of financial support. He goes on to quote Jesus in saying: "The worker deserves his wages" (v 18, quoting Jesus' words in Luke 10 v 7). Those who your church employs to teach and care and run the life of the church should be paid for by the rest of the church family; and so you should give to your church for that purpose.

We also see examples of support for "missionary" work—supporting the expansion of God's kingdom elsewhere. Paul says that the Philippian church has partnered with him in the gospel, meaning they have supported him financially (Philippians 1 v 5; 4 v 15-16). He also suggests that the Roman church might help in his planned mission to Spain (Romans 15 v 24).

So we are going to want to give towards this sort of work, both locally and internationally. This means helping support those in mission work, especially those sent from our own church. It might involve supporting those training for Christian ministry, new church plants, mission initiatives to reach a particular group of people who don't know the gospel, Bible translation, and more.

In practice, we should expect our giving to begin with our local church. That will usually involve the support of those who work for the church, care of those in the church, and mission work elsewhere. We may well stop at that, because in giving to our local church we will (hopefully) be giving to a variety of different needs as the church uses that money wisely. But many people can and will give elsewhere as well. That might be to a missionary that they know from a previous church, or to an aid project they have contact with. The danger of these "extras" is that our giving could go primarily to them, and not to our local church. There is a clear principle of giving to the church and the church then deciding how that money is spent. While we can't give figures, I think we can say that that's where the majority of our giving should go.

How much do we give?

This is an area that can be very simple or very complicated! It can be simple because some people give us a precise percentage—usually 10% of our income. This is called "tithing" (a "tithe" is a tenth).

So far, so simple. But once we look at what the Bible actually says about tithing, it becomes much more complicated.

Tithing is clearly commanded in the Old Testament. It was how people worked out what they should give to the support of the Levites (see Numbers 18 v 21-24). There was also a tithe that seems to have been for the festivals within Israel (Deuteronomy 14 v 22-27), and a tithe taken every third year for the support of the poor and also the Levites (v 28-29). These tithes were not optional—they were part of the law, and so not to give them was considered "robbing" God (Malachi 3 v 8-9).

There are debates as to how these different tithes relate and how they add up. Scholars calculate that they combine to give an annual figure of about 23% of a family's income; others come up with smaller figures, some slightly larger. But we live in a modern state, and not in Old Testament Israel; some of this money in Israel would have gone towards what is now covered by government taxes. Our situation is different in that our taxes already contribute towards care of those who are poor or ill (which should give a new meaning to taxes—they are part of caring for those around us).

The big question is: *Do we have to tithe?*

I think the answer is no. The tithe was part of the Old Testament law, and that law does not apply in the same way today. However, God presumably gave that law because it was a reasonable and workable amount. He thought that people could survive on the remainder of their income, and the same may well be true today. As a result 10% is probably a reasonable starting point—but it must not be regarded as either fixed or applicable in every situation.

We have seen something of the New Testament picture of giving above. It is driven by God's generous grace to us and calls us not to certain percentages, but to cheerful, sacrificial generosity. 10% might be very generous for some, but pathetically small for others. The New Testament approach is less one of "What must I give?", but more "What can I give?" If we grasp that giving is in response to grace, and is itself a grace from God, then we will want to maximise our giving, not limit it! And we need to remember that there were lots of examples of voluntary generous giving in the Old Testament as well as the laws on tithes (these were called "freewill offerings", e.g. Deuteronomy 12 v 6, 17). We will return to some practical guidance on what we spend on ourselves and what we give away in the next chapter.

Some of us would love to be given an exact percentage or amount we should give. That can be for good reasons because we want to know how to honour God. It can also be for bad reasons, so that we can feel we've done the right thing and feel pleased with ourselves. But the fact is we are not given such a figure.

We should notice that in the most extensive discussion of giving in the whole New Testament, in 2 Corinthians 8 – 9, there is no mention of tithes or any other figure. Rather the idea is to give as you are able and to do so freely and cheerfully. Paul is very clear that each person should give what they have "decided in [their] heart to give" (2 Corinthians 9 v 7) and we must not take that decision for each other.

But we should be honest with ourselves, and be able to discuss the issue among ourselves. If God commanded something like 10% in the Old Testament, it would be surprising if he didn't expect something similar for New Testament believers. Yet the truth is that if all church members actually gave 10% of their income, then most churches' giving would go up by some margin.

We need to be honest: if our income was reduced by 10% then the vast majority of us would actually manage life fine. And yet many of us think we can't afford to give that much. It is easy to think that we'll tithe, or give more generously, if we earn more, but statistics show that the proportion of giving usually reduces with increasing income. The biblical picture is that we might go without in order to give; not that we need to have more in order to give. This is not supposed to make us feel guilty but to prompt us to consider honestly what we give.

Giving in practice

How will we actually go about giving? Here are five guidelines:

1. Give thoughtfully

Sit down, think about it, and plan it. The point is that rather than giving on impulse, you decide thoughtfully how much you are going to give and who you are going to give it to. That doesn't mean you can't then give on impulse to a specific need as well, but it means you've worked out your giving plan. Many people need to set aside an hour to think, pray and decide. If you've not done that, get on with it!

2. Give regularly

For most of us, if we don't give regularly then we won't give what we intend. It is much better to set aside what it is to be given, ideally by giving it away or at least putting it somewhere specific (whether a different bank account or a different wallet). That action says: this is what I am giving so I'm not going to spend it. If we don't do this, then we're much more likely to give what happens to be left rather than what we plan to.

It will depend on what income you have and how you are paid, but it can be helpful to use automatic banking here. That way, giving will happen each month without your having to remember. Some Christian finance groups can be helpful too—money is given to an account with them, they reclaim tax, and then pay on to your church and elsewhere.

3. Give purposefully

Rather than giving simply because you know you should, give with intent. So as you give to your church, consider that you are supporting those who work for the church and allow them to do whatever teaching, leading or administrative tasks they do, you are giving to the missionary work, and the care work of the church. Money means ministry done or care given. So give to with those purposes in mind.

This is one downside of the automatic giving mentioned above. It can easily be that giving then happens without ever considering it—I certainly know that I have that tendency.

Probably the best solution is to pray regularly about and for your giving. Pray for those to whom you know the money is going; pray for the ministries it is supporting; pray for the care it is providing.

4. Give "secretly"

Jesus says:

> When you give to the needy, do not announce it with trumpets ... your giving [should] be in secret.
>
> (Matthew 6 v 2, 4)

We are not to display our giving to impress people. Giving is not to be done in a way that says, "Look at me and my generosity". That would mean putting cheques or cash in envelopes before handing them over in public. It would mean not looking to tell others about how much we give.

5. Give as a church

We are each part of a local church (or if we're not, we should be). We've already seen how our giving should be primarily to that local church for its support and for wider distribution. In that sense we give as a church to our common fund. But being part of a church comes into play in other ways as well.

Giving being secret shouldn't mean we don't talk about giving. We should speak about every area of the Christian life and do so in a straightforward way. There can be a danger that giving is never discussed because we think it's our personal business. Instead, we should want to help each other and encourage each other in giving.

We can go further. Because giving is part of our discipleship we should be able to challenge each other over giving. We cannot say to someone how much they should give—it should be what they have decided in their heart. But we can say they should give. And we can have honest discussions about what we give to and how much. In other words, we should be able to discuss the sort of material in this book together as churches. In doing so, we will be able to help each other gain or maintain right perspectives and encourage each other in good practices.

Questions for reflection:

1. Do you agree with the areas we should give to? Why or why not?
2. What do you think of tithing?
3. How do you go about deciding how much to give?
4. What should change in your approach to giving?
5. What should change in your practice of giving?

9. Living with money

We've looked at money and its deception... we've looked at the reorientation the gospel brings... we've looked at how we can get money wrong... we looked at living for true treasure... we've looked at how to guard against greed... and we've looked at giving. In this last chapter we want to draw all that together and ask: how do we live with money well in practice? How do we enjoy money without loving it? How do we live in a way that, in day-to-day life, avoids anxiety, idolatry and envy when it comes to money?

Loving with money

> "Love the Lord your God with all your heart and with all your soul and with all your mind." This is the first and greatest commandment. And the second is like it: "Love your neighbour as yourself." (Matthew 22 v 37-39)

These fundamental principles laid out by the Lord should guide all of life, including our use of money. They are the greatest and simplest summary of God's call on our life. So they provoke a simple but profound question: *Am I using money to love God and love people?*

That might sound as though we should give all our money to the church, or mission, or care of the poor. But it's not that simple in practice. Loving God means living in loyal devotion to him in all of life, living as he would want us to live. God expects us and wants us to buy food, to pay the bills, to get a haircut, to have a holiday, and so on. Loving God with our money doesn't mean we don't live a "normal life". But it does mean we approach normal life differently. We think of how we use money as a way we live for God, not how we look after myself. We think of spending money as doing what God would want us to do, not what we want to do. We do not think of our money as our own.

Imagine a parent giving some money to their teenage child for a holiday. They say: "Here's the money for travel, the accommodation and food, some for going out, and whatever else you need; use it wisely." The teenager heads off knowing they should pay their own way for the various costs of the holiday, but that they can also buy an ice cream. In fact, their parents would love it if they bought their friends an ice cream as well. And they would want their child to enjoy eating the ice cream, not feel guilty about it! That child should think of the money in their wallet as what their parents have given them to be used well according to what their parents would want.

That's how we should think of what we have. It is what God has given us to be used well. This means we live for God with our money by being responsible and paying our bills. We can and should also enjoy good gifts from him. We also show kindness to others and give money away.

So I can enjoy a good meal out and thank God for his gift and express my love for him. I can give money to people in need and thank God that I am able to do so. I can give money for the extension of God's kingdom and thank him for the privilege of being part of his work in the world.

This doesn't answer the question of whether I should buy

the music download I'd like, or go out to a restaurant next week, but it does give me an overall perspective: the money I have is money which God has given me to live life loving him and other people.

Choices to earn

Make it your ambition to lead a quiet life: you should mind your own business and work with your hands, just as we told you, so that your daily life may win the respect of outsiders and so that you will not be dependent on anybody. (1 Thessalonians 4 v 11-12)

Paul is picturing people working hard, earning money, and paying their way. He doesn't want people to be "dependent on anybody"; that is so that they don't need handouts. Again we see the value of work and earning money through work.

There can be lots of decisions about working. Circumstances may not give us much choice, but many of us will decide which sort of job to do, how long our hours will be, and in some cases whether to work at all (especially if we're married and our spouse works). Lots of factors feed into these decisions, but one is money. It is very easy to choose to work and to choose a certain sort of work because of what we'll be paid. That's not necessarily wrong as a factor. But let's be honest: we could easily choose to work, or spend more time working than we need to, because of the desire to earn more money, or to achieve a particular status. And we might choose to do that even though it will mean time not being used other ways: with family, serving within church or the community, developing friendships, and more.

A friend of mine swapped being a bus driver for becoming a taxi driver. Part of that decision was that he could earn more.

But he also considered the change in hours he would work and the impact on family life. Those factors mean that even if bus driver salaries went up, he should probably stay in the taxi business.

These decisions become especially significant in families. It is very easy for a couple to get used to having two incomes. They can buy a house or develop a lifestyle that requires both their incomes to sustain it. But assuming children come along at some stage, what will they do then? I don't think it's wrong for wives to work, but I do think full-time childcare is a very poor option that cuts against our responsibilities as parents. When we were first married, my wife and I decided to try to live on one salary so that we'd never miss her salary assuming we had children. Some of us may have to have two incomes to have a small home and enough food to eat, and it is not wrong to decide both parents will work. But many of us face the choice between making sacrifices and going without non-necessities on a single income, and enjoying an easier lifestyle on two incomes. Our children need our time more than they need money.

Of course, what options we have in what we earn will vary hugely between us. You may be frustrated by this section because you need to earn as much as you can just to get by; you may be saddened by it because health or circumstances mean you are currently unable to work; others will have the choice to work or not. The key issue to be honest with yourself and ask some good questions:

- *Why do I want to work?*
- *Why do I want to do this particular job or work this much?*
- *What financial needs do I, or we, have?*
- *Rather than assuming I have to earn to sustain my spending can my spending be reduced?*

Once we have an income of some sort, there are three things we can do with that money: spend it, save it or give it. Everything falls into those three categories, and we will probably do a mixture of all three. We'll think them through in turn.

Choices to spend

We will need to spend money! We pay taxes, need somewhere to live, and have to eat food. Most of us will spend most of what we earn each month—that's simply normal. We should be thoughtful about what we spend our money on, but we mustn't make a virtue of not spending.

How do we decide how much is OK, and on what? For most people I have spoken to, the hardest area is what I allow myself to buy when it comes to things I don't need. After all I'll live without that computer game, life will carry on fine without a new TV, not much will change if I continue to cycle my old bike, and I could just drink water.

We've already stated some guiding principles: we are to enjoy good things are part of God's creation, but we're not to be self-indulgent. We are to store up treasures in heaven, not on earth. We're to be rich towards God, not to ourselves. We're to love God and others with our money, rather than loving ourselves and our comfort or pleasure.

So when has spending gone wrong? How much is too much? From the day I was asked to write this book, I knew this was the question that would plague me! I knew it because I face that question myself, and I knew it because I knew how hard it is to answer.

The fact is there is no formula or rule to apply. We might like God to give us a green or red light on each purchase, but he doesn't. We might like it if our church could issue a budget of allowable spending, but they shouldn't. We must say it is a matter of wisdom. But we must also say it can be a matter of sin. We must take it seriously, because we could go badly wrong. But we must take it cautiously, because we could easily condemn ourselves or others wrongly. And we must also take it with a sense of perspective, because God doesn't want his people filled with angst over every purchase.

One approach I have found helpful is the way the seventeenth-century Puritan believers spoke about "moderation". They didn't deny the goodness of possessions and enjoying what money can buy; they saw them as good gifts from God. But they knew we could so easily get wrapped up in them, love them and live for them, start to store up treasures on earth. So they aimed at '"moderation". The idea is enjoyment and limitation.

What would that mean for today? It would include cutting out things we pay for but do not actually use and so are unnecessary—music that isn't listened to, owning a car that isn't really needed but is fun, sports club membership that isn't regularly used.

It would include putting limits on having too much of something. This is a difficult category to gauge. We quickly reveal our own priorities and what we think is worth spending money on. But we must reflect on this or we will simply go with our selfish preferences. So it might include owning a house that is bigger than our family or hospitality needs; buying luxury brands of food; always getting the latest gadget when the old one still works; going on expensive holidays.

Let me say immediately that I know even these suggestions are loaded with issues! How much is too much on a holiday? When does something count as a luxury? Again, there is no rule. But it is right that we think about these things, and recognise that some of us will tend towards limitation without enjoyment, and never spend; others will tend towards enjoyment without limitation, and make excuses for our spending.

How might we move towards this moderation? Here are a few questions worth asking about our spending:

- *Beware buying something simply because it is a good deal. Do you actually need it?*
- *Beware buying a higher quality item just because it's on sale: is it the best choice?*
- *Beware the temptation to keep up with the latest models or designs. Christians don't have to look like they bought all their clothes in the 1970s and use mobile phones from ten years ago. But we easily justify staying "up to date" when what we have works just fine. Has owning the latest model or fashion become an idol to us?*
- *Beware impulse buying. We're much better at considering what we actually need when sitting down at home rather than faced with a glossy product in the shop.*
- *Discuss purchases that are significant in terms of expenditure. Have conversations with members of the family and friends and ask: "Is this a good thing to spend money on?".*
- *For significant expenditure pause to ask: "What else could we spend this on? Would that be a better use of this money?"*
- *Beware instinctively thinking that having something new would make life better now. Think in terms of loving God and people, not enjoying things.*

Choices to save

Saving money is complicated, too! As with most things to do with money, saving is not wrong, but it can be. It turns on what we are doing, and why we are doing it. We might immediately think that the Christian with no savings is more godly because they are trusting God. And indeed they may well be. But they might not be saving because they are impulsive and enjoy spending.

It can be good to save for several reasons. First is for an anticipated future expenditure. You may plan an annual holiday, hope to replace furniture, or buy a new car. These tend to be larger costs that cannot fit into your usual spending. Saving for these is much better than borrowing and having to pay back interest.

Secondly, we might save for emergencies. Our car could suddenly pack up or be written off in an accident. Our house could need work done to it. Having some degree of "buffer" that softens the blows and means we don't have to go into debt is wisdom. And yet we can run into trouble here too—our hearts could easily love the idea of financial security and so trust what we have in the bank.

If saving is for emergencies, we can make some sort of estimate as to how much is suitable. But should that be the limit, or is it OK to save more and more if we are able to? Again, we can return to our question of "why"? Why are you saving more money? What is it for? Why not give it away now?

Thirdly, we might well also save by getting a pension. Pensions anticipate future need—a time when we cannot earn money—and so save for that time now. The alternative is to know that others will need to provide for us. That could be a decision a whole family makes: you all agree that no one gets a pension but everyone expects the children to provide for elderly parents. Pensions are not wrong—we can see them as a way to ensure we are not dependent when we do not need to be. But of course they can be! It all depends on our attitude: are we trusting the returns of our pension plan, or the care of our loving heavenly Father? Are we saving for a comfortable retirement full of expensive holidays and so on, rather than giving more and having a less luxurious future?

Lastly, we can save to give to our children. Paul makes an intriguing comment in writing to the church in Corinth:

> Now I am ready to visit you for the third time, and I will not be a burden to you, because what I want is not your possessions but you. After all, children should not have to save up for their parents, but parents for their children.
>
> (2 Corinthians 12 v 14)

Paul is talking about his relationship with the Corinthians, where he is like a father to them, and so he will give to them, not them to him. In expressing this, he implies that parents may well save for the sake of their children. We may save to help pay for education, or to buy them a car, or help with a down-payment on a house. Again, this could be done badly: it could be done at the expense of giving, with ungodly attitudes, and more. But it can be done well.

Not all of us will have much scope for saving, but many will. It can be a good and wise thing to do, and be done with godly motives. Or it can be done unthinkingly, presuming that more money in the bank is a good thing. Or it can be done selfishly and even idolatrously, putting our trust in money. We should ask:

- *What money am I planning to save?*
- *What am I saving for?*
- *Why am I doing this?*
- *What is my attitude?*

Choices to give

We can easily approach the questions of giving by asking "How much do I need to give?"

Alternatively, we could approach giving by asking "What do I need to live on?" We then only spend what we need, and give the rest to God. This is certainly a better starting point, but the drawback is that word "need". I could live on baked beans everyday and walk everywhere. How do I decide what I actually need? And what about enjoying anything good which is not strictly necessary? This quickly leads to the asceticism we saw in an earlier chapter.

A different approach I've been helped by is that of priorities. That is, I remind myself what I think is important in life. Those priorities should surely be:

- *Our relationship with God and love and worship of him*
- *Our relationships with and care of those of in our family*
- *Our relationships with other Christians in the community of the church, both local and global*
- *Our relationship with the rest of the world in mission and care*

We want to live lives around these priorities, including our giving, spending and saving. That might mean we rightly enjoy a good meal out with our spouse, or we buy a larger car so that we can take people with us on outings, or we extend our house so that we can have people over more easily. But equally we might not do any of those things because we want to raise money to support a mission partner.

Jamie Munson, in his book *Money: God or Gift*, gives the example of buying a big-screen TV. He imagines a Christian considering such a purchase. He could buy it for good reasons such as being able to invite friends over to watch TV together encouraging growth in relationships, and enjoying films and sport as a good thing himself. He could buy it for bad reasons: being embarrassed about the pathetically small TV he currently owns, or wanting to feel good about having the latest technology.

If he approached it from a "How much should I give?" point of view, then as long as he'd given his set amount he'd buy it if he could afford it. If he approached it from a "needs" point of view, he'd never buy it (or feel guilty if he did). A "priorities" point of view doesn't tell him whether to buy it or not, but helps him approach it the right way. He could decide to buy it for good reasons, or he could decide not to do so for equally good reasons.

We need to watch ourselves in at least two ways. First, we need to watch out for justifying expenditure on ourselves on the basis of "usefulness", such as buying the TV because it will benefit relationships. But second, we also need to watch out for condemning expenditure on the basis of "giving", such as saying buying the TV was wrong because that money could have been given away.

We must also return to the question of our hearts. We will continually struggle to know whether we are being indulgent or enjoying God's good gifts. We will wonder if we should give more and spend less. We must wrestle with these questions, but we must remember above all that what God is concerned about is the orientation of our hearts. The twentieth-century German pastor Dietrich Bonhoeffer wrote these challenging words:

"But where are we to draw the line between legitimate use and unlawful accumulation? Let us reverse the word of Jesus and our question is answered: 'Where thy heart is, there shall thy treasure be also.' Our treasure may of course be small and inconspicuous, but its size is immaterial; it all depends on the heart, on ourselves. And if we ask how we are to know where our hearts are, the answer is just as simple—everything which hinders us from

loving God above all things and acts as a barrier between
ourselves and our obedience to Jesus is our treasure, and
the place where our heart is."

Being different in our culture

We must be aware in this whole discussion that we are all hugely affected by our culture. That will play out in this whole area of spending, saving and giving. Our culture will tell us how we should spend and save, and the danger for us as Christians is that all we do is add some giving onto a standard amount of spending and saving. In other words, apart from some giving, my use of money looks no different to my non-Christian neighbour.

We must not simply take our cues from those around us; we need to critique our culture. John Wesley was a preacher in the eighteenth century. It was standard for someone of his social class to own silver plates and cutlery. When he had to fill in a return listing his income and possessions the tax commissioners wrote back to him, saying: "We cannot doubt but you have plate for which you have hitherto neglected to make entry." They assumed that he would own this silverware, or "plate", which was so standard. Wesley wrote back:

> *"I have two silver spoons at London and two at Bristol. This is*
> *all the plate I have at present, and I shall not buy any more*
> *while so many round me want bread."*

He stood out from his culture in not buying the expected silverware. There will be equivalents of that silverware for us, in our own communities and cultures.

So we need to ask:

- *What does my culture say I should buy? Is it right?*
- *What do adverts suggest I deserve? Do I?*

- *What do I learn about saving from those around me? Is that wise?*
- *Am I different to those around me? Why or why not?*

C.S. Lewis wrote in his book *Mere Christianity* that if our spending on luxuries is the same as those around us, we are almost certainly not giving enough away:

"If our expenditure on comforts, luxuries, amusements, etc. is up to the standard common among those with the same income as our own, we are probably giving away too little. If our charities do not at all pinch or hamper us, I should say they are too small. There ought to be things we should like to do and cannot do because our charities expenditure [giving] excludes them."

That is worth re-reading: it is very challenging, and very hard to argue with.

One way in which we can and should be different from western consumerist culture is not to expect our standard of living to go up as we go on through life. A man I know has decided what model of car he thinks is suitable for him to own. It is perfectly pleasant to drive but is certainly not a top of the range model. He will not buy a better car, even if his earnings rise and he can afford it. He'll keep that level of car, and give more away.

In other words, his priorities drive his spending. And his priority is not his own comfort or reputation. It is loving God and the growth of his kingdom; and loving his neighbour and their good. Perhaps this a principle for you to commit to: as and when your earnings increase, it will be your standard of giving, and not your standard of living, that goes up.

10. Give me...

You and I will spend the rest of our lives seeking to be wise in the way we handle the money God has chosen to give us. Sometimes we'll get it wrong and need forgiveness. Hopefully, often we'll get it right and please our heavenly Father. So as we finish, there are four things I hope you take from this book. None of them are rules. But all of them will help you to enjoy money without loving money much more than any checklist could do.

The perspective to want

We've seen that discipleship with our money is not simply about giving. It is about our perspective on all of life: what we are here for, what life is all about, what makes a life good. Life does not consist of our abundance of possessions; it is about being rich towards God. Life is not about the here and now, it is about God's kingdom which will last for eternity. Life is not about enjoying myself as much as I can on the way through but about loving God and people.

And this is the perspective that you and I need in order to put money in its place, so that we can use money without loving money.

The heart to have

We've seen that money is wrapped up with our hearts. It is very difficult to say that a decision to earn, save or spend money is absolutely wrong—it all depends on our hearts. Why are we earning, saving or spending? What is our attitude towards money—do we love it or God? Do we trust it, or do we trust God? Do we serve it, or do we serve God?

Pray that God will continue to renew your heart, and give you insight into the motives of your heart. You will need to continue to guard and watch your heart for all the subtle, and not-so–subtle, ways that it can be deceived.

The gospel to cling to

We've seen that our attitude to money is transformed by the gospel. God's grace changes us and leads us to be generous givers like him. The gospel teaches us what is important in life and realigns what we live for. To use money well, we need to keep on returning to the gospel.

We also return to the gospel every time we realise we've not used money well. When we've loved and served it; when we've been selfish or self-indulgent. We return to the gospel of grace where we know forgiveness and cleansing. We will continue to battle with our attitude over money as long as we live. We can make great progress, the battle lines can move forward, but the battle will continue.

And so you must continue to cling to the gospel. You are saved by grace, not by your good handling of money. Know the gospel, appreciate the wonder of the gospel, and let that gospel be what shapes you whenever you think about money—both yours, and others'.

The prayer to pray

There is a great prayer about money in Proverbs 30, and it is a great place to finish. It is very realistic about our hearts, and so wise in what it is asking for. Here it is:

Give me neither poverty nor riches,
   but give me only my daily bread.
Otherwise, I may have too much and disown you
   and say, "Who is the LORD?"
Or I may become poor and steal,
   and so dishonour the name of my God.

(Proverbs 30 v 8-9)

The wise person asks for neither poverty nor riches. They know that both have their dangers and will lead their hearts down a dangerous path. The danger of poverty is that I steal: I seek what I need wrongly out of desperation. The result is that I would bring dishonour to God.

But the danger of riches is that I "have too much and disown you". Asking "Who is the LORD?" is to say: *Who is this God that I need him or should pay attention to him?* The great danger of wealth is that I have so much money and possessions that I start to think I don't need God at all. I disown him, rather than rely on him.

The sixteenth-century Reformer John Calvin wrote of these opposite temptations:

"From the right are, for example, riches, powers, honours,
which often dull men's keenness of sight by the glitter
and seeming goodness they display, and allure with their
blandishments, so that, captivated by such tricks and drunk
with such sweetness, men forget their God. From the left
are, for example, poverty, disgrace, contempt, afflictions,

and the like. Thwarted by hardship and difficulty of these,
they become despondent in mind, cast away assurance and
hope, and are at last completely estranged from God."

If we know our hearts and the reality of temptation, we will ask God to give us neither poverty nor riches.

What will we ask for instead? "My daily bread." We will ask for what we actually need to get by. Not too much, nor too little, and relying on God for all of it. It is a request repeated by Jesus when he taught us to pray: "Give us today our daily bread" (Matthew 6 v 11).

It is a prayer that expresses trust in the God who cares for us and provides for us. We look to him to give us what we need. When faced with worries over our finances, we remember Jesus' encouragement not to worry because we are valuable to God (Matthew 6 v 25-26). He will give us what he knows we need; and he knows what we need far better than we do. And one day, he will give us all the riches of his eternal kingdom.

Give me neither poverty nor riches, but give me only my daily bread. That's the prayer of someone who loves the gospel of grace, who is letting the gospel shape their heart, and whose perspective on life and their future is dominated by the gospel.

So here's the big question: Is this a prayer *you* will pray?

Appendix One:
Debt, loans, mortgages and insurance

Loans and debt

The Bible recognises the reality of going into debt and doesn't think of it as a good thing. Proverbs tells us: "The borrower is slave to the lender" (22 v 7). When we owe people money we can too easily end up in their pocket. But having a loan and so being "in debt" is not necessarily wrong. There is such a thing as a responsible budgeted loan which I'll discuss below.

However there are real dangers involved here.

First, when we get a loan to pay for goods now or to cover expenses we have to pay interest on the loan. That means it will end up costing us far more than if we had saved up for the item before we bought it. This quickly becomes a foolish way of spending.

Secondly, our culture will encourage us to have items now which we cannot afford. "Buy now, pay later" has become a mantra of today. Offers of "Nothing to pay for two years" are common on purchases like large items of furniture or cars. Companies are happy to offer such deals because they know they'll get their money eventually. But the danger is we may not be able to pay for them when the two years are up. We easily assume we'll have the money at that stage, but unless we budget for it we probably won't.

Similarly, our culture encourages buying on credit. Credit cards have a high interest rate but a low minimum monthly repayment. Why? To encourage you to only pay the minimum and so have to pay a lot of interest. The result is many people end up with credit card bills gradually growing which they cannot pay off.

It has now become culturally normal to be in debt. A study in 2013 reported that the average household debt in the UK had doubled in the last decade. We are encouraged to spend by borrowing rather than saving and then spending. The result is that more and more of our spending is on repaying loans—which cost us more because of interest involved.

The section below will say more about responsible use of loans, but Christians must beware the encouragement of our culture to enjoy possessions now without being able to afford them. The result is unwise spending, and debt which we cannot get out of. (If you are in debt, look at Appendix Two on Resources for help—page 124.) We should surely want to honour God by only living within our income.

Mortgages and budgeted loans

We've been saying that we should live within your income. Only spend what you have, not what your bank will give you. We've mentioned the exception to this which is a responsible "budgeted debt"—that is, buying something we need now but cannot afford now. The obvious example is buying a house. It would take a very long time to save the money to buy something so expensive and we need to live somewhere in the meantime. So we can rent, or buy a house with a mortgage. This is clearly an example of "buy now, pay later". But it can be entered into as a loan we pay according to our means, just like we might pay the rent. The same can be true for buying a car. However, it is wise to ensure that the value of the house, or the car, is such that it could cover the debt if it were sold. There is a sense in which this isn't then real debt because the borrowing has gained you an asset which could pay off what you owe if needed.

That could apply to borrowing money to buy a TV, or new furniture. But these items quickly lose their value. So if we end up not being pay the loan back we can't sell the item to raise the money. And this clearly doesn't apply to borrowing money to go on holiday or cover extra expenditure at Christmas.

We cannot say that borrowing money is wrong biblically. But we can see the dangers of borrowing money and so do two things. First we try to avoid the buying now, paying later scenario, except where absolutely necessary. Second, when it is necessary we budget accordingly. We make the repayments part of our monthly payments. That is where monthly repayments are helpful because we know exactly how much we'll need to pay. One of the dangers with delayed payments is that I don't know how much I'll pay when. There's nothing wrong in principle, but lots of dangers in practice.

It might be that because of tragedy, illness or hard times you need a loan to pay for regular bills. It's not wrong to take one, but there must be a plan for how things will change in the future. If there isn't, then the cycle will continue and the debt will simply increase.

In general it's worth saying that loans for non-essential items are a bad idea. If we can live without something and save up to buy it later that's a much better route.

Insurance

We know we should not put our hope in money and we know we should rely on God to provide what we need. But what does that means for insurance? Our culture seems to believe that insurance is the answer for many financial problems—whether insurance for your life, your health, your TV, or your pet.

Some insurance is legally necessary, such as car insurance, or comes as part of a bigger package, such as house insurance as part of a mortgage. But most is up to us to decide. It ranges from large values such as home contents insurance, to tiny amounts such as an extended warranty on electrical devices. There is nothing wrong with insurance in principle. It is paying a small amount of money to have someone else take the risk of paying a large amount of money. Knowing how much a car tends to break down and what it costs to repair might mean I think it's a good idea to buy an extended warranty. The responsibility to provide for a family (1 Timothy 5 v 8) means we should consider life insurance so that if the earner in a family dies the dependents will be cared for. You can argue this is more necessary for younger families and those with grown up children may well decide to cease having life insurance. The point is that there is nothing wrong with these decisions in principle.

But there can, of course, be something wrong with our hearts—when our confidence and peace flow from our insurance policies rather than our loving heavenly Father. We must not believe the patter of the life insurance salesperson who makes it sound that our future is secure only if we buy this package. Our future is secure in God's hands; but it may be that one way he provides for us is through such a package.

There is also a danger of being unthinking in a culture that offers insurance with almost every purchase. We must remember that insurance companies make money! We pay them small amounts for them to take the risk of the larger amounts but we only make claims very occasionally. That means it is best to only insure ourselves for what we really cannot afford.

So consider insurance for things where the loss would leave you in debt rather than inconvenienced. For example, consider the extended warranty on electrical items. If your fridge broke you could probably afford to replace it. And you'd be much better placed to afford to replace it if you weren't paying for the warranty on the dozen other electrical items round the house. But if your house burnt down you'd struggle to replace everything in it. Here again we trust God and his provision rather than buying into the thinking that insurances really guarantees our future.

Appendix Two: Resources

Debt and budgeting

For those struggling with debt in the UK, I would recommend contacting Christians Against Poverty, who provide free debt management help (www.capuk.org). They also run a "Money Course" which helps with budgeting and handling your finances. Your local Citizens Advice Bureau can also give free guidance and help. In the US, Crown Ministries (www.crown.org) is a great place to start.

Giving

For help with regular giving as individuals (and also handling finances as a church) see Stewardship (www.stewardship.org.uk).

Books

Randy Alcorn, Money, *Possessions and Eternity*

Craig L. Blomberg, *Neither Poverty Nor Riches: A Biblical Theology of Possessions*

Craig L. Blomberg, *Christians in an Age of Wealth: A Biblical Theology of Stewardship*

Brian Rosner, *How to Get Really Rich: A sharp look at the religion of greed*

John Temple, *Family Money Matters: How to run your family finances to God's glory*

Paul Tripp, *Sex and Money: Empty pleasures, satisfying grace*

Appendix Three: A prayer for the rich

Here is a prayer about money. It is by a seventeenth century pastor called Samuel Hieron specifically for those who are rich—which of most of us in the Western world are, by global standards. I suggest reading, and praying, this slowly and frequently. It summarises much that we have covered in this book. It has done my heart good—I trust it will do the same for you.

My heart is loaded with much corruption and although riches be in themselves a blessing, yet without your special grace they will be to me a cause of many evils. They bring me to lift up my heart, to pride myself in my own conceit, to trust in my wealth, to despise others, to grow in love with this present world, to become cold and remiss in the best services, and to conclude that I am highly in your favour because you have enriched me.

These are the diseases which through the poison of our nature do rise by these outward possessions; neither can I say that my heart is clean from these corruptions. Purge them out of me I ask you, by the fiery power of your Spirit. Give me poverty of spirit and humility of mind, amidst this outward prosperity which you have given me. Make me remember that the more I have the greater shall be my account and the harder for me to be saved. By this may my wealth be so far from puffing me up with secure presumption, but rather move me to work out my salvation with fear and trembling.

Cause me to think often of the words of my Saviour, that riches are deceitful, and of a thorny nature, chocking the good seed of the word, and making it unfruitful. May I so learn carefully to handle them and to use them with great care and circumspection, lest I should by them wound my conscience and be pierced by many sorrows.

O let not my eyes be dazzled nor my heart bewitched with the glory and sweetness of these worldly treasures, which may be taken from me, or I from them, even in a twinkling of an eye. Draw my affections to the love of those durable riches and to the fruit of heavenly wisdom which is better than gold, and the revenues of which surpass the silver. Do this so that my chief care may be to have a soul enriched and furnished with your grace, filled with the knowledge of your will in all wisdom and spiritual understanding.

And because Lord in having much I am but a steward for you and a disposer of your gifts, enlarge my affection towards others, make me rich and fruitful in good works, being a father to the poor, and causing the heart of the widow to rejoice, warming the heart of the naked with the fleece of my sheep, not eating my meals alone but dealing my bread to the hungry and never hiding myself from my own family.

Why should I make gold my hope? Why should I strive to laden myself with this thick clay still plotting to set my nest on high, when all that I have, or can have, is in a moment turned into vanity? Quicken me up therefore to good duties, that the hearts of your saints may be comforted by me.

So Lord, shall I, by your goodness, have the true use of your blessings, together with a daily increase of much cause for thanksgiving, for your great goodness to me, vile and unworthy. All this for Christ and in his most glorious name. To whom with you and your Spirit, one true, everlasting, and only wise God, be all praise, power, might, majesty and dominion, now and forever. Amen.

A helpe unto devotion containing certaine moulds, or forms of prayer, fitted to severall occasions

thegoodbook
COMPANY
Opening up the Bible

At The Good Book Company, we are dedicated to helping Christians and local churches grow. We believe that God's growth process always starts with hearing clearly what he has said to us through his timeless word—the Bible.

Ever since we opened our doors in 1991, we have been striving to produce resources that honour God in the way the Bible is used. We have grown to become an international provider of user-friendly resources to the Christian community, with believers of all backgrounds and denominations using our Bible studies, books, evangelistic resources, DVD-based courses and training events.

We want to equip ordinary Christians to live for Christ day by day, and churches to grow in their knowledge of God, their love for one another, and the effectiveness of their outreach.

Call us for a discussion of your needs or visit one of our local websites for more information on the resources and services we provide.

Your friends at The Good Book Company

UK & EUROPE		thegoodbook.co.uk	0333 123 0880
NORTH AMERICA		thegoodbook.com	866 244 2165
AUSTRALIA		thegoodbook.com.au	(02) 6100 4211
NEW ZEALAND		thegoodbook.co.nz	(+64) 3 343 2463

 WWW.CHRISTIANITYEXPLORED.ORG
Our partner site is a great place for those exploring the Christian faith, with a clear explanation of the good news, powerful testimonies and answers to difficult questions.